audition speeches *for* 6 *to* 16 year olds

over 50 audition pieces for actors and actresses

SECOND EDITION

JEAN MARLOW

Bloomsbury Methuen Drama
An imprint of Bloomsbury Publishing Plc

B L O O M S B U R Y

LONDON · OXFORD · NEW YORK · NEW DELHI · SYDNEY

Bloomsbury Methuen Drama

An imprint of Bloomsbury Publishing Plc

Imprint previously known as Methuen Drama

50 Bedford Square	1385 Broadway
London	New York
WC1B 3DP	NY 10018
UK	USA

www.bloomsbury.com

BLOOMSBURY, METHUEN DRAMA and the Diana logo are trademarks of Bloomsbury Publishing Plc

First published in 2000
Second edition published in 2008
Reprinted by Bloomsbury Methuen Drama 2009, 2010, 2012, 2013, 2014, 2015, 2016, 2017

British Library Cataloguing-in-Publication Data
A catalogue record for this book is available from the British Library.

ISBN: HB: 978-1-4742-6101-2
PB: 978-0-7136-8772-9
ePDF: 978-1-4081-4106-9
ePub: 978-1-4081-4107-6

Library of Congress Cataloging-in-Publication Data
A catalog record for this book is available from the Library of Congress.

Series: Audition Speeches

Printed and bound in Great Britain

ıyard

audition speeches *for*
6 *to* 16 year olds

For Jennifer, Luke, Rosie, Holly
Micky and George

JEAN MARLOW

Frankly, I cannot think of a better person than Jean Marlow to be given the task of finding speeches for young actors.

From her early years when she played an astonishing sea lion in an impro for the Royal Court Theatre, until more recently when she was the leading Hen – 'Mrs Short-and-Long' – in *A Fox and His Drum* at the Unicorn Children's Theatre, she has retained a sense of fun – a sense of fun that stood her in good stead when she worked in Weekly Rep. Did they really have to learn a new play every week? (You can if the devil drives.)

Later, she became a presenter on commercial radio, interviewing pop stars and playing hits from the Top Twenty. She has also worked in many comedy series on television, and written and acted in films for the Children's Film Foundation. She played 'Mrs Jiniwin' in the Disney mini-series production of *The Old Curiosity Shop* and was 'Mrs Bunn' in *Whizziwig* – for Carlton Television.

She is Co-Director of The Actors' Theatre School and is the author of *Audition Speeches For All Ages and Accents, Classical Audition Speeches* and *Duologues For All Accents and Ages*.

EAMONN JONES
FOUNDER DIRECTOR
THE ACTORS' THEATRE SCHOOL

contents

LIST OF AUDITION SPEECHES

GIRLS 6–8

BOYS 6–8

BOYS 11–13

GIRLS 14–16

BOYS 14–16

acknowledgements

I would like to say thank you to the actors, directors, playwrights, casting directors, teachers, agents and organisations who have helped me with this book, and especially:

Carol Schroder, Brian Schwartz and the Offstage Bookshop, Jennifer Whelan, Jamie Dolan, Amieth Yogarajah, Tay Brandon, Kevin Daly, John Higgins, Kasia Coleman, Kieran Coleman, Luke Courtier, Rosie Courtier, Micky Churchill, George Syril Jnr., Holly Gibbs and the students from the Actors' Theatre School, Rona Laurie, Paul Todd, Jill Murphy, Gillian Diamond, Jaye Lewis, Heather Stoney, Maggie Lunn, Helen Curtin, Barbara Roberts, Katherine Adamenko, James Hogan of Oberon Books, Hilary Lissenden, Elly Crichton Stuart of Unicorn Children's Theatre, Samantha Iles of Alan Brodie Representatives, Samuel French, my Co-Director Eamonn Jones, the publishers A & C Black, Mark Dudgeon from Methuen Drama and my editors, Tesni Hollands, Katie Taylor and Jenny Ridout.

preface

Finding over fifty audition speeches for yonger actors has been a bit of an adventure – like taking on a dare. Could I actually find that many and would they be any good? Fortunately, I was helped by a group of young actors who not only suggested plays, films and books that they had seen or read, but tried out every single speech I selected to see if it worked. Some of these selections they used in their London Academy (LAMDA) or Guildhall Acting Examinations, or in end-of-term shows.

Each speech has its own introduction, with a brief outline of the story so far and a description of the character. All the speeches have been put together with children in mind, but I hope that parents and older actors will enjoy them and that teachers, in particular, will find them useful. The age-groups range from six to sixteen, but I could as easily have said from six to sixty as so many of these speeches are suitable for adults as well – especially those who work in Children's Theatre. 'Mole' in *Toad of Toad Hall* is in the six to eight age-group; but 'Moley' was played by actor Richard Goolden on stage and radio for over forty years. He was still playing the part in the West End at the age of eighty-five!

At the beginning of this book I have invited professional actors, playwrights, directors and casting directors to talk about their experiences working in children's theatre and television, and in some cases to give useful tips about auditioning.

It's been enormous fun searching out these speeches and talking to children's writers who have been so helpful and enthusiastic and who care such a lot about their work. My last great 'find' was the adaptation of *The Worst Witch*. There were two children with me at the time, and I wish everyone could have heard the cries of, 'Here comes the Worst Witch!' as the script came sliding out of my fax machine – and the book was complete.

introduction

in front of the whole class

Everybody remembers the first time they had to 'stand up and do something' in public: Mums, Dads, teachers, actors, pop stars, the Prime Minister – everybody. It could be reciting a poem you only learnt the night before in front of the whole class, singing a song at a party or saying your 'one line' at the end-of-term play. For some, it's a magic moment; others feel awkward or just plain scared.

I remember playing 'Miss Muffet' in a show given by my dancing school in a big hall over the top of the Express Dairy in the High Street. I was four. My Auntie had made me a special dress and I had a little blue bowl with gold stars on it. The class sang 'Little Miss Muffet' and I had to sit there eating my 'curds and whey'. But there was no spoon to eat them with and no spider. I felt really silly – I couldn't even join in the song because I didn't know the words. At the end, when the audience applauded half-heartedly, I joined in and applauded myself – banging my hands together as hard as I could because it was the only thing I knew how to do! 'Miss Muffet' taught me two important things about performing in public. Be sure you know your words, and always remember to check your 'props' before you go on stage – i.e. the spider my dancing teacher forgot to lower from the ceiling, and the spoon I left behind in the dressing-room.

Props
There are lots of opportunities at the beginning of this book for the very youngest of actors to learn to use props, whether real or imaginary. In *Alice in Wonderland*, Alice picks up the gloves and fan left by the White Rabbit and begins to fan herself. Pascal in *The Red Balloon* has a 'kitten' in a box; Zandile waves her 'stick' when she pretends to be the School Teacher talking to the flowers in her grandmother's garden.

'Learn the wordies'
A friend of mine once found himself sitting opposite a famous old actor on a tube train. He felt he had to speak to him, so he leaned across from his seat and said, 'I am a young actor just starting out in the theatre. What is the secret of your success? Can you give me any advice?' The great man replied, 'Learn the wordies, my boy! Learn the wordies!'

It's surprising how many people can't be bothered to 'learn the wordies' properly yet hope to get away with it! If I'd learnt the words of 'Little Miss Muffet' I could have sat there singing away happily with the rest of the class. Know your words. It's important. Just 'sort of' knowing them with your Mum hearing you go through them at home isn't enough. Know them inside-out and you'll feel a lot more confident.

'Can you hear me at the back!'

Some of you may already be attending stage school either full or part-time, and are not only entering for drama examinations but also being sent for theatre or television auditions. I'm sure that you've already learnt that the most important thing of all is: *Voice*. Can you be heard? If no-one hears you there is no point in doing anything. 'Street cred' is no good in a big space like a hall or theatre. If you don't say the beginnings or ends of the words clearly they just float off into a big 'nothing'. You don't have to sound 'posh' – just make sure everyone can hear you. Always play to the back of the theatre and the front will take care of itself. Or, as my teacher used to say, 'Remember little deaf old auntie sitting in the back row.' Don't rush your words. Most people speak too fast. They want to get the whole thing over as quickly as possible, so it all becomes a gabble. At last season's drama auditions a small girl came running out of the exam room screaming, 'Pig!' (I'm sure we've all felt like doing that at some time or other). The secretary explained very kindly to her parents that the examiner *had* to fail her. She had obviously tried to get her speeches over as quickly as she could and had gone far too fast!

Read the play

Although I've tried to give as much information as possible about individual speeches, you still need to read the play. Most plays can be borrowed from the library, and if the one you want isn't in stock they will order it for you or send you to another library that has got a copy. It is essential to find out as much as you can about your character. Ask yourself the following questions: What do the other characters say or think about my character? What does my character say or think about them? What does my character think about himself or herself? When was he or she born and in what period? Who is my character talking to – a friend or an enemy, a teacher or a parent? Make a list of your answers. These are the clues to your character and the key that can unlock the scene for you.

improvisation, theatre games and text

Improvisation and theatre games are important. They help to build up your confidence and develop imagination and self-expression. They are also great fun. Very often you are asked to improvise – that is, to make up a scene or create a situation – at an audition; but it is just as important to work on 'text' – the *written* words of a play or script – and have at least one good speech learnt that you can produce at a moment's notice!

A casting director complained recently about the number of young actors who are sent to see her without having anything they can perform, not even a short poem. 'An 11-year-old boy came in for an audition. He had no speech prepared and couldn't remember anything he had done. I suggested perhaps he could recite a nursery rhyme. I'll never forget having to prompt him on 'Humpty Dumpty'.'

sight-reading

If you are auditioning for theatre, films, television or radio – yes, even commercials – you are very likely to be asked to 'read'. This doesn't just mean burying your head in the script and mumbling away; it means trying to give the director or casting director an idea of the sort of performance you will give if you get the part. Don't let yourself be hurried or rushed into reading straightaway. Ask if you can have a minute to look through the lines. Then, when you are ready to begin, remember to try to look up as much as you can. This 'lifts the words off the page' and brings your performance to life.

Sight-reading takes practise, and there are lots of good speeches in this book to practise on. Reading aloud like this is also a very good way of finding a speech that you feel happy performing. It doesn't necessarily have to be in your own age-group.

a note for teachers and parents of younger students

Age-groups

As far as possible I have divided the speeches in this book into age-groups that I think can manage the demands of the particular text. However, these groups do not always match the actual ages of the characters. 'Albert the Mudlark' in *In Service* is described as very young and very small and so of course is the 'Dodger' in *Oliver Twist*, but both these speeches would be too difficult for most students in the six to eight age-group. 'Ernie' in *Ernie's Incredible Illucinations* is in the eleven to thirteen age-group, but my nine-year-old student, Jamie, loves this piece and is excellent when he becomes 'the boxing commentator'. Jennifer is also nine, but her favourite is the 'Grand High Witch' from *The Witches* and she's absolutely determined to use it for her next acting exam. So much depends on individual students, how advanced they are and what they like doing most!

Older age-groups

The speeches in the fourteen to sixteen age-group really come into the category of 'Young Adult' and would also suit students auditioning for drama schools and colleges.

Length of speeches

These selections are just about the right length for most examinations or auditions, unless there is a two-minute time limit specified; in that case they would need to be cut by perhaps a third. Some of the speeches in the six to eight age-group are a little long, but this is because I didn't want to shorten them and spoil the story! There is no reason why they shouldn't be cut. 'Tabitha' in *Tom Kitten and His Friends* can easily finish her speech when she tells her kittens not to 'have anything to do with the Puddle-Ducks', and 'Duchess', the dog in *The Mystery of the Pie and the Patty-Pan* could finish on the line, 'I really couldn't eat a mouse pie.'

children's theatre

The majority of speeches in this book are taken from plays written for children and young people: *The Lion, the Witch and the Wardrobe*, *The See-Saw Tree* and *The Wild Swans*, among many others.

Alan Ayckbourn, Artistic Director of the Stephen Joseph Theatre, Scarborough and one of our busiest and most popular playwrights and directors, has this to say about the importance of children's theatre:

'I immensely enjoy writing plays for children, or really for what I prefer to call the 'family' audience, because it's probably as hard if not harder than writing for adults. You have to be more aware. Children won't lie to you – they judge you immediately. They can get bored very quickly. Adults are polite people normally and if something is a little boring, they'll sit and watch it and think, 'Well, it'll get more interesting in a minute.' But children just go, 'Boring!' and turn round and talk to their friends. All the things that matter in any sort of theatre matter twice as much for children. Good story, good dialogue, characters you are interested in. My imagination really catches fire sometimes! To write for such an audience sharpens your playwriting skills no end. It's affected my adult work, I know. In fact, one such play, *Wildest Dreams* – quite a frightening play – is in one sense entirely a children's play. I'd never have written it if I hadn't experienced the thrills and spills of writing for the younger audience. The shame in this country, of course, is how little importance is attached to children's theatre. It's appallingly underfunded – the companies that do exist providing quality work all year round survive on a shoestring. There are many excellent writers producing scripts for children, as is apparent from this book, but there should be many more. But how can there be when they receive precious little monetary reward and hardly any critical acknowledgement?

Young people are the theatre-goers of tomorrow, but if they're never given the chance to see exciting, innovative and imaginative theatre in their childhood, how can they develop an interest in watching plays in their adulthood? If we're not careful, they will be lost forever to television, cinema and all those special effects. They will never have experienced the joy of watching something 'handmade' especially for them in one particular place on one particular day. That's what the 'liveness' of theatre is about and what we have got to *keep* alive.'

about auditioning

It's always interesting, and often useful, to hear about young actors getting their first professional job – sometimes from an end-of-year showcase and sometimes from an interview or audition. And so I've asked two actors who began their careers when they were still at school, to talk about how they got their first 'breaks'.

FRANCE CUKA, a Royal Shakespeare and Royal National Theatre player, tells us how she became a child star on the radio.

'It was the long summer holidays. I was twelve, and bored, so I wrote to the BBC, offering them my services. I told them that I had had elocution and acting lessons, my singing voice had a range of three octaves (it was true at the time), and that I could also produce a light tenor voice if required. I was convinced that they really needed me, so I was a little miffed when I got a reply asking if my letter was meant to be taken seriously. I answered that indeed it was, and some time later I was asked to audition for *Children's Hour*. This programme went on every day from 5.00–6.00 p.m., and had short plays, stories and chats for young people. It was very popular.

The first thing I did for them was a serial of an American family going west in a covered wagon. I played the whiney youngest daughter forever saying, "It's not fair" in a high, shrill voice and generally being a pain in the neck. I also took a tiny part in episode one, of the baby brother. On reaching episode four we found that my two parts had a scene together, so I did a scene with myself!

I did *Children's Hour* through the rest of my schooldays, despite continually having to see the Headmistress to be asked when I was going to give up this "nonsense", and through my time at drama school as well. They always paid me the same, three guineas. No wonder they used me, I was dead cheap!

Later, while in a hit play in the West End, they offered me the lead in a Saturday Night Theatre, at the same money. My agent demanded a great deal more, to get the astonished answer, "She always took it before!"'

MARGO SELBY – 'Julie Corrigan' in BBC Television's *Grange Hill* – was trained at the Sylvia Young School and played in the Royal National Theatre's production of *Cat on a Hot Tin Roof*. Margo has also appeared in *The Bill*, *Eastenders*, and played the lead and sang the title song in *Flying Dream* – a children's film about dinosaurs.

'When I was little – before I started acting – I used to get bored and was often very naughty. I would spend hours singing songs from musicals, and used to pretend that I had played the lead in the film of *Annie*. "I know I look different now," I'd say, "but that's the camera for you, and it *was* filmed a couple of years ago!" I would tell everybody this. I was only eight at the time, and I actually thought I had them fooled. Yes, I was very precocious. Being sent to stage school at the age of nine was a dream come true, and I was surrounded by loads of children who had the same passion for performing as me.

I remember my audition for *Grange Hill* very clearly. I walked into the room and fell flat on my face. I then stood up and asked in a giggle, "Do you want me with or without my glasses?" I wasn't shy and I looked the auditioners straight in the eyes. I think this helped me, apart from the fact that I looked right for the part of the school "victim". I was a short, round redhead with glasses – plenty of scope for the bullies!

In nearly all my auditions I have had to read scripts that I hadn't seen before for more than about five minutes. I soon realised that it was essential to be able to read really well. This is important because it allows your character and acting skills to come through in a relaxed and "real" way. I can remember auditioning alongside children who were having difficulties reading the script. They may have been fantastic on screen, but their reading stifled their chances of proving this. The other thing I always found important to keep in mind was, if you are asked to try the part in a different way, be sure to make a point of presenting a *big contrast*. It shows that you are open to direction and can listen and react well with the director.

Smile and have confidence. Good luck!'

what are directors and casting directors looking for?

Who are the people you are likely to meet when you audition for theatre, films, television, radio or commercials? They can be casting directors, producers, directors or writers or, in the case of commercials, advertising agents and their clients. Most important of all, what are they looking for? Most young actors I've talked to say it would be really helpful if they could have some advice from the auditioners themselves, as well as perhaps a few tips on the 'do's and don'ts' of auditioning.

CLAIRE TOEMAN – The Crocodile Casting Company
Crocodile is Claire's own company, specialising in casting TV commercials. She works with actors, models and children and has been a Casting Director for twelve years. Before this she was an actor, so she has experience on both sides of the camera. She enjoys her work, as every day is a different challenge.

'If you attend an audition for a commercial you need to remember that the advertising agency in charge of writing and making the commercial, is looking for the right face to sell their product.

When you arrive you will probably find lots of other children at the audition, all of a similar age and appearance to yourself! Don't be put off – the most important thing is that you enjoy your audition as much as you can. If there is a script, and sometimes there isn't, read it carefully. You will be given an improvisation to do and will often go in to the audition room or studio in a group of other children.

The improvisation may be silly – you may be asked to give various expressions to the camera, or perhaps pretend to eat a bowl of cereal. If you are with a group, don't monopolise the conversation and equally as important, don't be shy or you might not get noticed at all.

There may be a lot of people in the casting room, as well as the director, cameraman and casting director – and often people from the advertising agency will come along. This can be a bit distracting as ad agency people are sometimes speaking on their phones or eating lunch, so you need to concentrate hard on what the director is telling you.

The audition process for commercials is always quick, but the wait to go in can be a long one, so make sure you are not hungry, especially if you have come straight from school. If you have been asked to wear a certain style of clothing it really helps if you can dress as requested.

After the audition is over, go home and forget about it! If you are lucky you may hear that you have been short-listed for the job. Don't get too excited. A short list can sometimes be a long list, especially with commercials! If you get the job that's fantastic, if not . . . never mind there will be other opportunities.

The main thing is to be yourself, and if you do get lucky don't get big headed. Some years ago I cast a young boy in several commercials and he began to get very big headed. Then he came to see me for another casting . . . He walked into the studio, I asked him how he was and he picked up my newspaper and hit me over the head with it! Needless to say I sent him back to his mum pronto and told her I wouldn't be seeing her son again until he learned to behave himself!

So . . . be warned and good luck!'

EDWARD WILSON, former Director of the National Youth Theatre, has this advice to give:

'Auditioning is for some possibly the most terrifying thing they ever have to do – worse than a visit to the dentist, or being chased by a shark!

Unfortunately it's rarely possible to give your best in a state of extreme nervousness. I think the most important frame of mind for anyone auditioning is to genuinely enjoy the piece you're performing and try to convey your own enjoyment to the person who is auditioning you. Always be as confident as you possibly can about knowing the words, because the fear of drying up is in nine cases out of ten the root cause of nervousness in the first place. So study properly!

Never go along to an audition laden down with costumes or props. Nothing is more boring and time-consuming for an auditioner than to have to wait whilst someone either dresses up for the part or arranges an entire furnished room around themselves before they can even begin to perform their piece. None of this is necessary and it certainly won't put the auditioner in a good frame of mind. Similarly, very few auditioners like to be spoken at, or involved in some way with your performance. It makes it impossible to observe what you are doing properly. So focus your attention elsewhere.

Above all remember that whilst it might be a very important thing to succeed in an audition, it is not a matter of life and death. So enjoy the experience and you'll probably achieve more success.'

Award-winning television script writer **RICHARD CARPENTER**, remembered for his *Catweazle* series and more recently *Robin of Sherwood*, *The Borrowers*, and *The Scarlet Pimpernel*, started out as an actor. He has strong words to say about auditions and auditioning:

'I used to hate auditions because I always thought of all the others that had auditioned before me. And I used to feel sorry for the people holding the auditions. How bored they must get – especially if it's the same piece over and over again. "What," I used to think, "are they looking for? Good acting? Something out of the ordinary? Someone who looks like me? Or someone who doesn't?" Trouble is, you don't really ever know. And whoever sent you may have got it wrong. They may be looking for someone older. Or younger. Or taller. Or shorter. And there's not a lot you can do about that. There's the famous story of the playwright who sent an actor friend of his to an audition for one of his plays. "I've written the part for you," he told him. The actor was bald but he had a very nice wig which he wore for the audition. The director called out to him from the darkness that they were looking for someone bald. Quick as a flash the actor removed his wig. There was a pause. Then the director's voice floated up to him over the footlights. "Er, yes," he said, "but I don't see you *playing* it bald."

So remember this: however good you are – however well you do your audition – if they don't want you, you won't get the part. And it won't be your fault.'

A producer or director is just as anxious to cast the right actor for the part as you are to get the job. Producer and director **NEVILLE GREEN**, responsible for the popular *Whizziwig* series for Carlton TV, has also produced *Mike and Angelo*, *Poltergeist*, and the award-winning film, *Never Rest*. He explains the problems of casting and talks about working with children in television.

'It's a headache. It's a heartache. It's a joy. Just a few of the emotions and physical conditions one experiences when working on productions for children and with children.

It's a headache; caused when you can't seem to find, identify, or cast the right child actor for a part in a production after having interviewed, smiled and chatted with what seems like hundreds of children (probably in reality twenty to thirty at the most) – all bright, enthusiastic and intelligent but not one of them that seems suitable for the part.

The heartache; caused by having to reject and turn down children for reasons that are very often nothing to do with them or their ability, but more to do with one's own sense of believing what the part and character should be. No matter how a rejection is said, instantly at the audition – or more usually through their agent – you can still sense the hurt. One can only hope that the maxim, "children are resilient and will bounce back" is the truth.

It's a joy; is pretty obvious. The right child with the right personality has been found and will be a joy to work with.

Working with children is also exceedingly taxing. They are very enthusiastic, energetic and very excited about the production, and they are very interested in all aspects of the technical and creative side of productions. Because of the advent of television and more recently computers, they have a greater concept and awareness of how film and television work and are made, so their questions and interest are much more intensive and knowledgeable. This keeps a director on his toes and up to scratch with the latest electronic and digital effects and techniques. An answer to their questions of, "Er, well, this is an, er, thing that does that, er, good isn't it!" will not satisfy their quest for knowledge.'

RICHARD CALLANAN is a producer and director who has specialised in children's drama. His credits include: *Adam's Family Tree, Little Lord Fauntleroy, Maid Marian and Her Merry Men* and *Jay Jay the Jet Plane.* He was Executive Producer of children's drama at the BBC from 1988 to 1996.

TEN DON'TS FOR AUDITIONS

(1) Don't dress for the part
It's tempting, but it will usually be seen as 'naff'. Working clothes are best – the kind that you can happily rehearse in and that will give you freedom of movement. Wear comfortable shoes too – three-inch high-heels for girls are rarely a good idea. (If you think it might be a good idea, you can always bring them in a bag.) Girls who know it's a costume drama may want to wear a skirt rather than jeans or leggings, but make it a comfortable skirt that you can move in if you are asked to.

(2) Don't audition with your mouth full
Most adults hate chewing-gum. They feel insulted if you talk to them while you chew and it never (well hardly ever) fits with any part you are looking for.

(3) Don't insist on talking too much
Those auditioning you want to get to know you and what you think. So when they ask you a question they hope for more than 'Yes', 'No' and 'Boring'. Don't go to the other extreme either – don't keep on telling the story of your last holiday in Marbella. If you are being auditioned with other kids at the same time, don't hog the spotlight – make sure you don't try to dominate.

13

(4) Don't fight with other children waiting with you

Waiting for auditions can be very tedious and uncomfortable. The room where you will be asked to wait will probably not be a proper waiting room. It might be overheated and overcrowded. Tempers can get edgy. Resist the temptation to snap at someone waiting with you; they may be rivals, but they can't help it. And try not to sulk if you think things are going badly. Bad behaviour as you wait may be noticed and give you a reputation of being difficult.

(5) Don't flirt with the director

This is a message for everyone who auditions – of both sexes and any age. Directors (or good directors, anyway) are not interested in flirting. For them auditions are a difficult and demanding process. The success or failure of their project may depend on doing it well. Flirting is not funny or clever. And remember there is usually more than one person involved in casting; a producer, for example, who sees you flirt with a director is unlikely to be impressed.

(6) Don't let your mother, father or 'minder' bully you

Controlling your 'minder' is never more important than at audition. If they are seen to be too pushy it will count against you. Of course, they must feel free to be able to ask questions; but even if they do have to wait around longer than expected, try and get them to keep smiling and not complain out loud.

(7) Don't wait until you are called to go to the loo

Yes, it happens! Kids could be waiting for an hour for their turn, and then – just as they get called in to audition – they ask to go to the loo! Producers and directors like to think of themselves as very busy people so make sure you go before you are called.

(8) Don't hide

The director and his team want to see you. If you are in a group, don't go behind other people, flee to the back of the area or turn your back. It may be natural to the action some of the time but make sure you don't do it continuously.

(9) Don't cover your eyes with your hair

The eyes are the focus of communication. If your eyes cannot be seen when you turn sideways you are losing a major means of expression, so make sure your eyes can always be seen – both of them if possible. (Girls with long hair who wear it up may have another problem. It may make you look older or too sophisticated. If you do wear your hair up, make sure you can let it down easily if asked.)

(10) Don't boast about your dad or mum

It's *you* who are trying to get a part, not your parents. It's you who has to be impressive, not them. So don't say, 'My dad is the drummer in Spiky Sausage.' The likely reply you will get is, 'So what?'

So – now you know! (JM)

BARBARA ROBERTS, Children's Casting Director for the Royal Shakespeare Company, Stratford-upon-Avon, has this to say about auditioning.

'When I am auditioning here at the Royal Shakespeare Theatre, I usually organise some kind of group warm-up before seeing everyone individually. It helps to break the ice a little, and also gives us a chance to watch such things as movement, etc. in a more relaxed atmosphere.

In the audition itself we are looking for confidence above all – if you are confident you can get away with anything! (Well, almost!) Be as natural as you can and avoid being "stagey".

It is quite useful to have a couple of audition pieces learnt already, then to polish one up when you have an actual audition. A well-rehearsed audition piece stands out from the rest; it shows in your performance that you have taken the time and effort to work on it.

I know how nervous some of you will be, but remember you will have a very short time to show us what you are capable of. Try and put your nerves on hold and enjoy the experience. Make the most of it, and above all, go for it!

Lots of luck.'

CAROL SCHRODER, LLAM, is an Examiner for the London Academy of Music and Dramatic Art (LAMDA) and an experienced teacher of drama and performing arts. She has written several textbooks.

'All children enjoy acting. In this new collection of audition speeches for children, there is a delightful variety of suitable material. Teachers will find that these scenes meet the requirements of many performing arts courses and in particular the LAMDA examinations.

As a teacher I enjoyed the inclusion of some familiar characters for very young children and also the adaptations from well-loved books. In all the selections the characters are clearly defined and the scenes are imaginative, which will encourage acting skills.

Writers working in the theatre today are also represented by some stimulating and challenging scenes for both boys and girls. All the texts chosen give opportunities for young actors to explore character, movement, voice and use of space.

As an Examiner I commend this inventive collection of material. I am sure it will prove to be a useful resource book for young performers and their teachers, leading to some creative and successful performances.'

audition
speeches

Alice – aged 7

ALICE'S ADVENTURES IN WONDERLAND
LEWIS CARROLL

ALICE had been feeling very sleepy, sitting beside her older sister on a grassy bank with absolutely nothing to do, when she saw a White Rabbit, dressed in a waistcoat and pocket-watch, go hurrying past her. She followed the Rabbit, who disappeared behind a bush and into a large rabbit-hole. **ALICE** went tumbling down after him, and that was the beginning of her adventures in Wonderland.

In this scene **ALICE** is in a long, low hallway. She has eaten a cake marked, 'Eat me' picked out in currants, and has grown so big that she is unable to get through the little door that leads to Wonderland. She begins to cry and turns to see the White Rabbit, this time splendidly dressed, carrying a pair of white gloves and a fan. When he sees **ALICE** he drops the gloves and fan and scuttles away. **ALICE** picks them up and starts to fan herself as she speaks.

Published by Macmillan Publishers Ltd, London

Alice

Dear, dear! How queer everything is to-day! And yesterday things went on just as usual. I wonder if I've been changed in the night? Let me think: was I the same when I got up this morning? I almost think I can remember feeling a little different. But if I'm not the same, the next question is, Who in the world am I? Ah, *that's* the great puzzle! . . . I'm sure I'm not Ada, for her hair goes in such long ringlets, and mine doesn't go in ringlets at all; and I'm sure I can't be Mabel, for I know all sorts of things, and she, oh! she knows such a very little! Besides, *she's* she, and *I'm* I, and – oh dear, how puzzling it all is! I'll try if I know all the things I used to know. Let me see: four times five is twelve, and four times six is thirteen, and four times seven is – oh dear! I shall never get to twenty at that rate! . . . I must have been changed for Mabel! I'll try and say '*How doth the little –*'

> *How doth the little crocodile*
> *Improve his shining tail,*
> *And pour the waters of the Nile*
> *On every golden scale!*
> *How cheerfully he seems to grin,*
> *How neatly spread his claws,*
> *And welcomes little fishes in,*
> *With gently smiling jaws!*

I'm sure those are not the right words . . . I must be Mabel, after all, and I shall have to go and live in that poky little house, and have next to no toys to play with and oh! ever so many lessons to learn! No, I've made up my mind about it; if I'm Mabel, I'll stay down here! It'll be no use their putting their heads down and saying 'Come up again, dear!' I shall only look up and say 'Who am I, then? Tell me that first, and then, if I like being that person, I'll come up: if not, I'll stay down here till I'm somebody else' – but, oh dear! . . . I do wish they *would* put their heads down! I am so *very* tired of being all alone here!

Zandile – Black South African – aged 8

HAVE YOU SEEN ZANDILE?
GCINA MHLOPHE, MARALIN VANRENEN
AND THEMBI MTSHALI

First performed at the Market Theatre, Johannesburg in 1986 and also as part of the Edinburgh Festival at the Traverse Theatre in 1987. It is set in the sixties and is based on Gcina Mhlophe's own life. **ZANDILE** lives with her grandmother in Durban, a bright child who dreams of growing up to become a teacher – until her world is turned upside down when she is kidnapped by her natural mother and expected to conform to the ways of life in the harsh, rural Transkei homeland. In this scene **ZANDILE** is only eight years old. She is in her grandmother's garden speaking to the flowers as if they are a class of children and she is their teacher. She has a small stick in her hand.

Published by University of Kwa Zulu-Natal Press

Zandile

Ho ho ho ho! Good morning class! Good morning, Miss Zandile. And what was all that noise I was hearing down the passage? Poor Miss Bongi could hardly teach her Standard Twos. She teaches Nature Study, you know, she's very clever. But do you know what happens to naughty children? The white car will come for you and you won't even know it's coming. It's going to be standing there and it will be too late to run. Nobody can hear you scream because its engine makes such a loud noise. They're going to take out your eyes and take you to a far away place and nobody's going to see you ever again. *(She pauses as if she is listening to something)* And what is that I'm hearing . . . is that the white car? Ho ho ho ho! No, you are lucky this time. But I'm going to send you straight to the principal's office and he is going to give you this *(she demonstrates a hiding with her stick)*.

Don't you know what day it is today? It is the 21st of September 1966 and the inspector is coming here today. You know the inspector does not understand our language *(she starts giggling)* and we don't want to embarrass him. *(Puts her hand over her mouth and laughs)* He cannot say our real names so we must all use white names in class today. Hands up those of you who don't have white names. We'll just have to give them to you. Wena you can be Violet. *(She points to different sections of the audience each time she mentions a different flower)* Petunia. Daisy. Sunflower and Innocentia . . . I don't know what that means . . . Do you know what name the inspector gave me in class today? Elsie. And I don't even look like an Elsie! Don't laugh! At least you are flowers. And do you know what he called Bongi? Moses! He couldn't even tell that she is a girl.

21

Lucy

THE LION, THE WITCH AND THE WARDROBE
C.S. LEWIS

Dramatised by Adrian Mitchell

First performed in 1998 at the Royal Shakespeare Theatre, Stratford-upon-Avon and transferred to the Barbican Theatre, London in 1999.

This is the story of four children, **LUCY** (the youngest), Susan, Edmund and Peter, who are evacuated to the country during the London Blitz. Exploring the attic in their new home, **LUCY** discovers an old wardrobe – it is the gateway opening out into the Land of Narnia. Narnia is under the spell of the wicked White Witch and the four children find themselves caught up in an adventure leading up to a final struggle between the powers of good and evil.

In this scene, **LUCY** takes the other three children to meet her new friend, the faun Mr Tumnus. On arriving at his cave she finds that it has been ransacked and there is a notice saying that Mr Tumnus has been captured and is about to stand trial on the charge of 'comforting Her Majesty's enemies and fraternising with Humans'!

Published by Oberon Books, London

Lucy

We'll see Mr Tumnus first. He's the faun I told you about. Come on, then. This way. I'll go in first! Oh! *(The door has been wrenched off its hinges)* Mr Tumnus! *(LUCY plunges into the cave) (Off)* Oh no! Mr Tumnus! . . . *(LUCY emerges slowly, sadly carrying a wrecked painting)* Poor Mr Tumnus. It was a lovely cave . . . It's as if somebody dropped a bomb. Everything's broken – all the plates and cups. And this painting of Mr Tumnus' father – it's been slashed to pieces by somebody's claws. *(She throws it back into the cave)* . . . I found this notice pinned up. *(Reads from paper)* 'The former occupant of these premises, the Faun Tumnus, is under arrest and awaiting his trial on a charge of High Treason against her Imperial Majesty Jadis, Queen of Narnia, Chatelaine of Cair Paravel etcetcetc, also of comforting her said Majesty's enemies and fraternising with Humans. Signed MAUGRIM, Captain of the Secret Police. LONG LIVE THE QUEEN!' . . . She's not a real queen. She's the White Witch. All the wood people hate her. She cast a spell over the whole country so that it's always winter here. Always winter but never Christmas . . . That poor faun's in trouble because of me. He hid me from the Witch and showed me the way home. That's what is meant by comforting the Queen's enemies and fraternising with Humans. We've got to rescue him! . . . Look! A robin! It's the first bird I've seen here. I wonder if birds can talk in Narnia? *(Addressing the robin)* Please can you tell us where Tumnus the Faun has been taken? *(LUCY takes one step towards the bird, who flies to the next tree)* He wants us to follow him.

Rosie (8 years old)

MY MOTHER SAID I NEVER SHOULD
CHARLOTTE KEATLEY

First produced at the Contact Theatre, Manchester in 1987 with a revised version premiered at the Royal Court Theatre, London in 1989.

The play moves back and forth through the lives of four women, Doris, Margaret, Jackie and Rosie from 1905 (when Doris was only five) to 1979.

Scene Ten is set in Raynes Park in September 1979. It is ROSIE's eighth birthday and she comes into the garden carrying an old spoon and Margaret's doll Suky (from Scene Two set in 1940 when Margaret was nine). It is a baby doll, now bald except for a few tufts. She proceeds to bury the doll under the cherry tree.

(At the end of the scene Jackie sees the old spoon and scattered earth and digs Suky up again.)

Published by Methuen Drama, London

Rosie

It's my birthday today and it's all gone wrong already. I'm going to bury you, Suky. Eight is too old for dolls. I want a Sex Pistols T-shirt. Some hope. Unless Jackie brings me one! I'd have buried you ages and ages ago, Suky, if you hadn't been Mum's. I couldn't care less now if Mum sees me doing this. *(Digs in the tub)* Suky. Stupid name. Even cutting your hair off it won't go punk. I bet Mum cuddled you and stuff, didn't she? Well I only hug people when I want to, not when it's visitors. *(Holds doll over her face. Pause)* When I want to I can hug harder than anyone. In the world. *(Pause)* I'm saving it. *(Pause. Digs hole. Lowers the doll over it, then holds it closer to her)* I was going to give you away to the toy collection at school, d'you know that? Mummies give their babies away sometimes. They do. *(Pause. Slowly lays the doll in the hole)* Shut up crying. There, see, I'm putting you in this urn. People get buried in urns. *(Covering the doll over with earth)* Jackie'll be here soon. She never cries. No one else at school has a sister who's a grown-up. I might easily run away with Jackie and live with her. Then you'd be sorry, Suky. So would Mum. *(Suddenly bright, as if enormously relieved)* I'm going to paint the cherry tree now – for Jackie.

Duchess – a little dog

THE MYSTERY OF THE PIE AND THE PATTY-PAN
BEATRIX POTTER

Dramatised by Rona Laurie

DUCHESS, a little dog, receives an invitation from her friend, Ribby, a pussy-cat, to come and have tea with her. Ribby has baked a very special pie for her in a pie dish with a pink rim, but **DUCHESS** is suspicious about the pie's contents. She would much prefer to eat her own veal and ham pie, baked with a little patty-pan in the middle. In this opening scene, **DUCHESS** has just been handed a letter by the postman.

(*Note* This scene provides a good opportunity for young actors to work with props and practise both reading and writing a letter on stage.)

Published by Puffin Books, London

Duchess

A letter for me? Thank you, Postman. *(She opens the letter and reads it)* 'Dear Duchess, will you come to tea with me today? Come in good time, my dear Duchess, and we will have something so very nice. I am baking it in a pie-dish – a pie-dish with a pink rim. You never tasted anything so good! And *you* shall eat it all! I will eat muffins, my dear Duchess!' *(Then she goes into her house and writes a reply. Writing and reading aloud)* 'My dear Ribby, I will come with much pleasure at a quarter past four. But it is very strange. I was just going to invite you to come here, to supper, my dear Ribby, to eat something most delicious. I will come very punctually, my dear Ribby.' *(She pauses to think for a moment and then adds)* 'I hope it isn't mouse?' That does not look quite polite. *(She scratches out 'isn't mouse')* 'I hope it will be fine.' *(She goes to her front door, sees the postman passing her gate and gives him the letter)* Will you please deliver this to Mrs Ribston? *(She goes into her house and reads Ribby's letter again) (To herself)* I am dreadfully afraid it *will* be mouse! I really couldn't, *couldn't* eat mouse pie. And I shall have to eat it, because it is a party. And *my* pie was going to be veal and ham. A pink and white pie-dish! And so is mine; just like Ribby's dishes; they were both bought at Tabitha Twitchit's. *(She goes into her larder, takes the pie off a shelf and looks at it)* It is all ready to put into the oven. Such a lovely pie-crust; and I put in a little tin patty-pan to hold up the crust; and I made a hole in the middle with a fork to let out the steam – Oh I do wish I could eat my own pie, instead of a pie made of mouse! *(She goes to her table and reads Ribby's letter again)* 'A pink and white pie-dish – and *you* shall eat it *all*.' 'You' means me – then Ribby is not going to even taste the pie herself? A pink and white pie-dish! Ribby is sure to go out and buy muffins . . . Oh what a good idea! *(She jumps up, delighted with her own cleverness)* Why shouldn't I rush along and put my pie into Ribby's oven when Ribby isn't there?

Tabitha – a mother cat

TOM KITTEN AND HIS FRIENDS

Based on a story by Beatrix Potter
Play by Adrian Mitchell

First performed at the Unicorn Theatre for Children in 1995, *The Tale of Tom Kitten* is one of four adaptations of stories under the main title.

A mother cat – **TABITHA** – is expecting her friends to tea and is determined that her three kittens, Mittens, Moppet and Tom will look their very best.

In this scene she comes out of her house to call them in from the garden.

Published by Samuel French, London

Tabitha

Stop playing, Kittens! Tom and Mittens! Stop it, Moppet! . . . I am expecting friends to tea. So come indoors immediately. I must dress you before the fine company arrives. (TABITHA *chases the kittens indoors*) . . . So my visitors say: What fine kittens you are: (*She sings – combing* Tom)

> *Take a spiky little comb*
> *To your whiskers and your tail . . .*

(Tom *scratches* TABITHA. *Shocked, she licks her paw*) Tom Kitten you should be ashamed of yourself. Come, Moppet and Mittens – put on your clean pinafores and tuckers . . . Now Thomas, I have all sorts of elegant clothes to dress you up in. (*Pushing him into his suit*) You shall wear your sky-blue suit. Hold out your arms. Breathe in, Thomas. Oh dear. There goes a button . . . There! You're done. Now all three of you are beautiful. But I want you all to be out of my way while I make hot buttered toast. Out you go, into the garden! (*She pushes them out*) Now keep your frocks clean, children! You must walk on your hind legs. Keep away from the dirty ash-pit, and from Sally Henny Penny and from the pigsty. And don't have anything to do with the Puddle-Ducks. *(She goes back into her kitchen and busies herself making toast) (She sings)*

> *We have a little garden*
> *A garden of our own*
> *And every day we water there*
> *The seeds that we have sown.*

(TABITHA looks out of the door) Mittens! Moppet! Tom Kitten! Whatever do you think you're doing – sitting on the garden wall with no clothes on? *(She pulls them off the wall and cuffs them and drives them back indoors)* There'll be no hot buttered toast for you. My friends will arrive for tea in a minute, and you are not fit to be seen. I am affronted. Yes, I am affronted. *(The kittens are shooed out of sight)* What have I done to deserve such kittens? Still, the garden's looking at its best for my visitors. *(The church clock chimes four)* Four o'clock. Tea-time. And here come my friends. *(Her three friends come into the garden)* There's hot buttered toast for everyone. *(She brings out a tray piled high with toast and tea)* My children are all upstairs in bed. They are unwell. They have measles. In fact they're totally covered in spots. Yes, absolutely, under their fur. Do sit down, friends. It doesn't do to keep hot buttered toast a-waiting.

Whizziwig – an alien

WHIZZIWIG
MALORIE BLACKMAN

Published in 1995, Whizziwig was a children's serial.

WHIZZIWIG is a small, friendly alien whose space-ship has just crash-landed on Ben's roof. She is described as more 'girl' than 'boy' – but then they don't have girls or boys on their planet. Ben has complained to his Mum and Dad that a small furry thing is bouncing about in his bedroom, but they tell him to lie down and go to sleep. The bouncing continues.

In this scene WHIZZIWIG appears for the first time on top of Ben's wardrobe and insists on introducing herself.

Published by Puffin Books, London

Whizziwig

My name is Whizziwig. I am sorry if I frightened you. I did not mean to. I would have spoken to you before, but it has taken me this long to learn all the spoken languages on this planet . . . I'm on top of the wardrobe. Can I come down now? (WHIZZIWIG *bounces down from the wardrobe and bounces towards* Ben's *bed)* I am an Oricon. What the people on your world would call a wish-giver . . . I was passing your planet four days ago on the way to visit my auntie, when some space debris hit my ship and I had to make an emergency landing on your roof . . . It is still up on your roof. It will have to stay there until I can fix it. (WHIZZIWIG *sighs)* I have been bouncing around this immediate area ever since I arrived and I have yet to fix a single thing . . . It will take wishes to fix my ship. And I can only fix it by giving people whatever they wish for . . . I can't give you a new bike. (WHIZZIWIG *rocks to the left and then to the right)* Nope . . . I can only grant wishes if you make a wish for someone else . . . You have to wish almost without realising what you're doing – it has to be unselfish wishing . . . That's the way it works . . . I am an accidental wish-maker . . . There are different types of Oricons. Some make dreams come true, others make daydreams come true, some give you exactly what you want, some give you the exact opposite of what you want. I grant wishes – but only to those who make wishes for someone else . . . that is my job. It is tough, but someone has to do it!

Fairy

THE WILD SWANS
HANS CHRISTIAN ANDERSEN

Adapted by Rona Laurie

This is the story of Eleven Princes who are turned into wild swans by their wicked stepmother, and their sister, the Princess Elise, who runs away into the forest in search of them.

In the forest Elise meets an Old Woman who gives her some berries and tells her where the wild swans are living.

In this scene Elise has found her eleven 'swan' brothers, and lies down to sleep with the youngest swan's head resting in her lap. In a dream a **FAIRY** appears to her with stinging nettles in her hand, and tells Elise what she must do to save the Princes – weave eleven long-sleeved shirts from stinging nettles, despite the pain of picking them, and throw one over each swan. All this must be done in complete silence; one word from Elise, and her brothers' lives will be forfeit.

Fairy

Do you remember the old woman who gave you berries in the forest? I was that old woman, in disguise. I have come to tell you how you can free your brothers from the Queen's wicked spell. But it will not be easy. Have you courage and patience enough? Your tender fingers will feel burning pain and your heart will be tormented with grief. Do you see these stinging nettles in my hand? They grow around this place where you are sleeping. But only those which grow here or on the graves in churchyards are of any use. Remember that. You must pluck them though they sting your hand. *(The FAIRY touches Elise's hand with a nettle)* You must trample them with your feet and get yarn from them and with this yarn you must weave eleven shirts with long sleeves. When they are all made, throw them over the eleven wild swans and the spell will be broken. They will become human again. But remember this, Elise, from the moment you begin your work until it is finished you must not speak a word. If you do, the first word that you speak will plunge like a dagger into the hearts of your brothers. Their life depends on your silence. Remember this! *(She drops a nettle by Elise's hand and exits)*

Loll – Gloucestershire

CIDER WITH ROSIE
LAURIE LEE

A stage adaptation by James Roose-Evans

Performed at the Hampstead Theatre in 1963 and later transferred to the Garrick Theatre, London. The poet, Laurie Lee, remembers scenes from his childhood in a Cotswold village.

In this scene, Laurie Lee, known as **LOLL** to his family and friends, is sitting in school waiting for the arrival of the new Headmistress, Miss Wardle. As she enters, he sniffs and is immediately told to go outside and give his nose a good blow.

Published by Samuel French, London

Loll

[LOLL *sniffs . . . he leaves the classroom area and sits on the very edge of the stage]* Of course I don't really belong to that lot at all. I'm summat different to them. I'm a – I'm a – young king. Yes! Placed secretly here in order to mix with the commoners. *(He sniffs)* There is clearly a mystery about my birth. One day the secret will be told. One day, they'll see, a gold coach with footmen in uniform will turn up suddenly, just like that, outside our kitchen door, and our Mother will cry and they'll stand very solemn and respectful to our Marge and Doth and Phyll and Jack and Tone, and then I shall drive off to my palace. I shall eat bacon and eggs off my throne. Course I shall be generous. I won't throw my brothers in a dungeon. No. Instead I shall give them a banquet of cakes and jellies and – things! And all my sisters, our Marge, our Doth, our Phyll, they shall have princes and they shall live in a palace in . . . *(His imagination runs out here)* Where shall it be? Ah yes. Stroud! . . . *(The children in the classroom rise swiftly and start singing the national anthem, conducted by* Miss Wardley]

[**Chorus** *(singing)* God save our gracious King . . .]

. . . And when I am King, Miss Wardley shall curtsy!

(He joins the rest in place, singing loudly, aggressively)

[**Chorus** *(singing)* Long to reign over us, God save our King!]

(All sit)

Billy

THE GIRAFFE AND THE PELLY AND ME
ROALD DAHL

A play with music for children, adapted by Vicky Ireland

Commissioned by Polka Theatre for Children, Wimbledon, London and performed by them in 1992.

BILLY longs to see 'The Grubber' – a deserted sweet-shop near his house – returned to its former glory. His dream seems impossible until he meets a strange trio of animals, the Giraffe, the Pelly and the Monkey, also known as 'The Ladderless Window-Cleaning Company'.

In this opening scene, **BILLY** introduces the audience to 'The Grubber' and we meet the Giraffe for the first time.

Published by Samuel French, London

Billy

Hallo. My name's Billy. Not far from where I live, there's something very strange. It's a house. Not an ordinary house, but a strange old one made of wood. It stands by itself on the side of the road. *(The lights go up on The Grubber at back of the stage – a sign on the window reads 'For Sail')* Look, there it is. *(He walks carefully up to the house and reads the sign on the window)* 'For Sail' . . . Hmmmm. It's been like this for ages, all empty and shut up. Wish I could get in and explore, but the door's always locked . . . *(Looking through the window)* It's all dark and dusty inside, but I know the ground floor used to be a shop, because look, you can still just read the lettering up there, it's a bit faded, over the window . . . 'The Grubber' . . . ? *(Mum enters)* Mum . . .? What does the word 'Grubber' mean, do you know – the word that's over the shop? . . . A sweet-shop! . . . Wow! So that's what it was. It must have been a lovely old sweet-shop. Oh, I wish I could buy it . . . then I'd make it into a grubber all over again. I'd do anything to have my own sweet-shop. Just think, Mum, what it would be like . . . Caramel Fudge – that'd be grand . . . Sugar Pig Snorters . . . Butter Gumballs? . . . *(To audience)* But the next time I went to visit 'The Grubber', something had happened – something exciting . . . somebody had scraped off the 'For Sail' sign, and painted instead – look – 'Soled'. Soled! I was too late. Now that old sweet-shop would never be mine . . .The next day I was back. Hey, look at the door, it's changed, it's fantastic. Hang on, no-one could use a door like that except a giant. *(Reading the window sign)* 'The L-ladder-less Window Cleaning Company . . . Get Your Windows Cleaned Without a Lot of Dirty Ladders Leaning Against Your House.' What on earth's it all about! *(One of the windows on the top floor begins to open outwards)* Just a minute, something's happening. Oh crumbs! *(The Giraffe's head appears at the window)* Wow!

Hansel

HANSEL AND GRETEL
JEAN MARLOW

An adaptation from *Grimm's Fairy Tales*

Grimm's Fairy Tales were written by the Brothers Grimm in 1812 and were collected from German folk tales, popular stories of that time and ancient manuscripts.

HANSEL and his little sister Gretel, live with their father and cruel stepmother in a small cottage on the edge of the forest. Food is very scarce and the family is almost starving. Their stepmother has always disliked the children and persuades their father to take them deep into the forest and leave them there. That evening he sets off with the children on the pretence of collecting wood. He gives **HANSEL** a crust of bread tied up in a red-spotted handkerchief. **HANSEL** is suspicious and as they walk further into the forest he breaks up the crust of bread, leaving a trail of crumbs behind them. When they reach the deepest part of the forest, their father tells them he must leave them for a while but will be back to fetch them later.

In this scene the children are becoming anxious. It is nearly an hour since their father left them and Gretel is starting to cry.

Hansel

Don't cry Gretel. Father didn't mean to leave us all alone in the forest. I know he didn't . . . please don't cry! *(He takes a red-spotted handkerchief from his pocket and shakes it out)* See. I've broken up the crust of bread he gave us and left a trail of crumbs leading all the way back home again. Think how happy he'll be when he finds us all tucked up and snug in our beds tomorrow morning. *(He laughs)* Look! The moon is coming up from behind the clouds and we can easily find our way back. See – there are the breadcrumbs. They start from here and they go all along the path and . . . Oh no! The trail has stopped . . . Of course, the birds have eaten them up! There's only little bits left. And I simply can't remember the way back . . . Never mind, father will come and find us very soon . . . Don't worry, I'll look after you . . . How beautiful everything looks in the moonlight . . . And over there I can see a little house. I wonder if there's anyone at home. Come on. Let's go and see. *(They hurry towards the house and then stop and sniff)* Mmm! What a lovely smell! Like the gingerbread mother used to bake! *(They move in closer)* It *is* gingerbread! It's covered in gingerbread! And look! The stones around the door are little cakes! *(He goes up to the front door and raises the door knocker)* Chocolate! The door knocker's made of chocolate. *(He breaks off a piece and starts to eat it – then frightened, he jumps back)* What's that? I thought I heard something . . . No, it's only the wind. *(He creeps up to the door again)* Look, Gretel. The windows – they're made of barley sugar. *(He breaks off a piece of window-pane and hands another piece to Gretel. The front door opens suddenly and an old lady pokes out her head at them)* Oh! . . . I'm sorry! I didn't mean to break your window. But we were so hungry . . . We haven't eaten all day . . . I'll buy you a new door knocker . . . And my father will put in a new pane of er – barley sugar for you . . . Please forgive us!

Pascal – played in the film by a 5-year-old boy
THE RED BALLOON
ANTHONY CLARK

Adapted for the stage from a film by Albert Lamorisse

First performed by the Contact Theatre, Manchester and then by the Royal National Theatre in 1996. It is set in Paris in 1956 and tells the story of **PASCAL**, a lonely little boy who is bored at home and tormented at school, until he makes friends with a big red balloon.

PASCAL's classmates have snatched his satchel, broken his new pen and torn up his homework book, then run off leaving him all alone in the pouring rain. He sees a kitten crying in the street and unable to find out who it belongs to, takes it home with him. He names it 'Hercule'.

Next morning **PASCAL**'s mother insists that he takes 'Hercule' back to where he found him. **PASCAL** sulkily collects a cardboard box and lifts the kitten into it. His mother asks to see his homework and in this scene he tries to explain what has happend to it. He leaves the house with 'Hercule' in the box. On his way down the street he meets his friend 'Raggedy' the Tramp. 'Raggedy' likes cats and **PASCAL** persuades him to take care of 'Hercule'.

Published by Oberon Books, London

Pascal

It was an accident. It was raining, and I was running to get home, and I dropped my book, and it fell open, and the page with my homework on fell in a puddle, and all the ink ran, and then I tore out the page because I didn't want to ruin the whole book . . . I promise you, it's true . . . And I dropped my pen . . . And the nib broke . . . I couldn't help it Maman. Everything fell out of my satchel. I had to protect Hercule from the rain. Cats don't like water do they? I had to put him in my satchel, and then I wanted to keep my books dry, so I put them under my jersey. But they wouldn't stay and they kept falling out . . . *(PASCAL puts* Hercule *into the box)* Come on Hercule, or we'll be late. Say goodbye . . . Hercule say 'thank you'. Maiow! . . . *(He leaves)*

(The street. A Tramp *is asleep beside an old dustbin. The* Tramp *stirs. Enter* PASCAL *with* Hercule *still in the cardboard box)* You don't remember him, do you? Do you remember me? . . . Yesterday . . . He was crying in the rain. Cats don't like the rain . . . I'm not allowed to keep Hercule, because I live in a flat. And Maman and Papa don't like cats, though they pretend they do. Papa says he'll ask the concierge if I can keep Hercule, but he'll forget. He always does. And Maman said it's not fair. Can you look after him for me? He's never a nuisance. He likes playing all the time. I'll bring you my scraps for him to eat. He doesn't eat much, he's got a very small stomach. Please? Just until Mama and Papa stop arguing, and Papa stops worrying about money, and he remembers to ask the concierge to change the rules . . . Don't lose him, will you? . . . Be careful . . . See you soon Hercule. Raggedy, will look after you.

Jay

THE SEE-SAW TREE
DAVID WOOD

First performed by the Farnham Repertory Company in 1986 and then at the Sadler's Wells Theatre, London, in 1987.

The See-Saw Tree is a large oak tree inhabited by its animal residents – Owl, Squirrel, Mistlethrush, Bat, Cuckoo, Dunnock and **JAY**. We see them going about their business, tidying their nests, feeding their young and chattering happily with their neighbours, until the dreadful news that the tree is to be sawn down to make way for a children's playground.

In this early scene **JAY** is hopping from branch to branch selling his suitcase of wares to the local housewives. These include dried grasses, badger hair, sheep's wool and even polythene bags and bits of paper. His first customer is Mistlethrush. He announces himself as 'Travelling salesbird supreme'.

Amber Lane Press, Charlbury, Oxfordshire

Jay

(Suddenly JAY arrives – on the branch below, near Squirrel's *drey. He is brashly confident, and carries a kind of 'suitcase' for his wares)*
What music fills my ears? . . . Such tone. Such pitch. Such artistry . . .
Jay's the name, madam. Travelling salesbird supreme . . . I have been on a flight of exploration, madam, spreading my wings far and wide in search of marketable merchandise. Scouring the countryside for new and exciting lines to offer my lucky customers at bargain prices. What do you fancy? . . . Aha! See my selection, perfect for the use of. *(He opens his coat. Inside his wares are neatly displayed)* Dried grasses, bracken, quality mosses, badger hair, sheep's wool for extra warmth, polythene and paper. Pick your own, mix 'n' match, yours for the modest sum of two acorns. Can't say fairer than that . . . Do me a favour . . . Aha! Think ahead, madam. Think of when your eggs hatch. Think of all those hungry little beaks to feed. No problem. *(He opens the other side of his coat, revealing more merchandise)* I've got crab apples, juicy slugs, calorie-stuffed caterpillars, mouthwatering worms, specially selected spiders, meaty maggots and crunchy moths. Take your pick . . . Your loss, dear lady, not mine. Happy laying.

Kay

THE SNOW QUEEN
HANS CHRISTIAN ANDERSEN

Adapted by Jean Marlow

There was once a wicked goblin who invented a magic mirror so powerful that whatever was reflected in it appeared hideous and distorted. All the other goblins thought it a huge joke and planned to fly it up to heaven and make fun of the angels there. But as soon as they got near to heaven the mirror began to shake so much that they had to let go of it and it came crashing down to earth and shattered into millions and millions of pieces. These tiny splinters of glass went flying all over the world. Some of them flew into people's eyes, so that whatever they looked at appeared hateful to them. Other splinters pierced their chests, turning their hearts into blocks of ice.

Two children, **KAY** and Gerda, lived next door to each other high in the rooftops of a small Scandinavian town. They were the best of friends. **KAY** would often spend the afternoon with Gerda and together they'd listen to her grandmother telling them fairy stories. **KAY**'s favourite story was always the one about the snow queen.

In this scene it is winter and as **KAY** looks out of the window, the snow is beginning to fall.

Kay

(Looking out of the window) Gerda! Come and see! It's starting to snow again. Look at the snowflakes – how beautiful they are. Each one is different. *(He holds his arm out of the window to catch a flake on the sleeve of his jacket)* See – this one is like a marvellous flower, or a star – a ten-pointed star. They're much more beautiful than real flowers. It's snowing faster now – the flakes are getting really big! They're whirling about and swarming like white bees. Do you suppose they have a queen like real bees? Your grandma says they do. She says that when the snowflakes start to swarm, the queen is always there – the Snow Queen. *(Leaning out of the window)* Oh how I wish I could see her. I don't believe she is a real queen at all. I'd like to catch her. Then I'd make her sit on the hot stove and watch her melt! *(He laughs – then suddenly turns from the window)* Oh! – I've got something in my eye. *(He rubs his eye)* And there's a pain deep in my heart. Like a needle stabbing me. *(Gerda goes to put her arm around him)* It's alright – it's gone now. It doesn't hurt any more . . . *(He pushes her away)* Why are you crying? What a stupid ugly girl you are. And you look even uglier when you cry. And your voice – it's horrible – like that old crow that sits up on the roof. 'Caw, caw.' *(He imitates Gerda's voice)* 'Oh poor Kay. Where does it hurt? Caw! Caw! Caw!' *(He takes up a stick)* And I hate these flowers in their stupid pots. I'm going to knock their heads off. *(He hits out at the flowers. Gerda tries to stop him)* Leave me alone! Or I'll knock your head off too! *(He runs over to the window and looks down into the street)* The snow is getting deeper. I'm going out to play. No you can't come with me. I'm going to take my new sledge. And I'm going to go tobogganing with the other children in the square!

Mole – any age

TOAD OF TOAD HALL

A play from Kenneth Grahame's *The Wind in the Willows* adapted by
A.A. Milne

First produced at the Liverpool Playhouse in 1929, it is based on the
adventures of the foolish Toad and his friends: the kindly Rat, the
wise Badger and the gentle, but very nervous, **MOLE**.

This scene takes place at night in the middle of the Wild Wood –
a frightening place in the moonlight – with the snow thick on the
ground. **MOLE** comes limping in through the trees, looking over his
shoulder as he hears the mocking laughter of the creatures who
inhabit the wood. His friends had warned him not to come here and
now he is hopelessly lost.

Published by Samuel French, London

Mole

(Hopefully) Ratty! *(In sudden panic as a bat crosses the stage)* What's that? Pooh! It's nothing! *I'm* not frightened! . . . I do wish Ratty was here. He's so comforting, is Ratty. Or the brave Mr Toad. *He'd* frighten them all away. *(He seems to hear the sound of mocking laughter)* What's that? *(He looks round anxiously)* Ratty always said, 'Don't go into the Wild Wood.' That's what he always said. 'Not by yourself,' he said. 'It isn't safe,' he said. 'We *never* do,' he said. That's what Ratty said. But I thought I knew better. There he was, dear old Rat, dozing in front of the fire, and I thought if I just slipped out, just to see what the Wild Wood was like – what's that – ? *(He breaks off suddenly and turns up stage, fearing an attack from behind. There is nothing)* I should be safer up against a tree. Why didn't I think of that before? *(He settles himself at the foot of a tree)* Ratty would have thought of it, he's so wise. Oh, Ratty, I wish you were here! It's so much more friendly with two! *(His head droops on his chest)* . . . *(waking up suddenly)* What's that? . . . *(frightened)* Who is it? . . . *(Rat enters and crosses to* MOLE. *He has a lantern in his hand and a cudgel over his shoulder.* MOLE *is crawling around distraught, almost in tears)* Oh, Rat! . . . Oh, Ratty, I've been so frightened, you can't think . . . *(sitting)* Oh, Ratty. I don't know how to tell you, but I'm afraid you'll never want me for a companion again, but I can't, I simply *can't* go all that way back home now . . . I'm aching all over. Oh, Ratty, do forgive me. I feel as if I must just sit here for ever and ever and ever, and I'm not a bit frightened now you're with me – and – and I think I want to go to sleep.

Boy

THE WITCHES
ROALD DAHL

Adapted by David Wood

First performed at the Lyceum Theatre, Sheffield in 1992 and then at the Duke of York's Theatre, London.

BOY and his grandmother are staying at The Hotel Magnificent, where the Witches are holding their annual meeting, supposedly of The Royal Society of the Prevention of Cruelty to Children. It is presided over by the Grand High Witch, who is planning to 'rub out' every child in England with her latest formula, which will turn them all into mice. This potion is to be injected into tasty sweets and chocs. A greedy boy, Bruno Jenkins, is also staying with his parents at the hotel and becomes her first victim. BOY, who has been searching for his missing pet mice, William and Mary, has wandered into the ballroom where the meeting is being held and quickly hides behind a screen. But the Witches smell him out and force him to drink the rest of the potion.

In this scene, BOY comes scampering back into the ballroom as a 'mouse'. He sniffs around, calling for Bruno. He meets Bruno, now also a 'mouse', eating a chunk of bread. At first Bruno refuses to believe what has happened to him and then begins to cry. BOY tries to explain the advantages of being a mouse and then plans their escape.

Published by Penguin, London

Boy

(Calling) Bruno! Bruno Jenkins! *(No reply.* BOY *frisks around happily. To the audience)* I should be sad. I should feel desperate. I mean, I've never dreamed of being a mouse, like I've dreamed of being, say, a film star. But now that I *am* one, I'm beginning to see the advantages. I know mice sometimes get poisoned or caught in traps but boys sometimes get killed too – run over or get some awful illness. Boys have to go to school. Mice don't. Mice don't have to pass exams. When mice grow up they don't have to go out to work. Mmm. It's no bad thing to be a mouse. I'm as free as William and Mary. Hope they're all right. (Bruno, *dressed as a mouse, enters eating a chunk of bread –* to Bruno) Hallo, Bruno. (Bruno *nods)* What have you found? . . . An ancient fish paste sandwich. Pretty good. Bit pongy . . . Listen, Bruno. Now we're both mice, I think we ought to start thinking about the future . . . (Bruno *stops eating)* But you're a mouse too, Bruno . . . Look at your paws . . . Don't be silly, Bruno. There are worse things than being a mouse. You can live in a hole . . . And you can creep into the larder at night and nibble through all the packets of biscuits and cornflakes and stuff. You can stuff yourself silly . . . Maybe your rich father will get you a special little mouse-fridge all to yourself. One you can open . . . We'll go and see my grandmother. She'll understand. She knows all about witches . . . The witches who turned us into mice. The Grand High Witch gave you a chocolate, remember? . . . Follow me to Grandmother's room. Down the corridor, run like mad . . . No talking. And don't let anyone see you. Don't forget that anyone who catches you will try to kill you! . . . Come on.

Arrietty
THE BORROWERS
MARY NORTON

First published in 1952, and made into a BBC Television series adapted by Richard Carpenter in 1992.

Beneath the floor behind the kitchen clock live a family of tiny people; Pod and his wife, Homily, and their young daughter **ARRIETTY**. Everything they have, clothes, furniture, food and even their own names, are borrowed from the human 'beans' upstairs, and they call themselves 'The Borrowers'.

Pod has been seen as he was climbing down the curtains, by a human 'Boy', while he was on his last borrowing expedition. The time has come to warn **ARRIETTY** about human 'beans' and how danger-ous it is to venture upstairs alone. Over supper, Pod and Homily tell her how her cousin Eggletina – who had never been told about the dangers of 'Upstairs' – had climbed up there on her own and never been seen again. Her father, Uncle Hendreary, was broken-hearted, and he and his family emigrated very soon afterwards. It was thought that the cat had got Eggletina.

Published by Puffin Books, London

Arrietty

Why did you tell me this? Now? Tonight? . . . You think they'll get a cat? *(She sets down her cup of soup)* Couldn't we emigrate? . . . Supposing that I went out, like Eggletina did, and the cat ate *me*. Then you and papa would emigrate. Wouldn't you? *(Her voice falters)* Wouldn't you? *(Her eyes fill with tears)* I was only thinking that I'd like to be there – to emigrate too. Uneaten . . . It's not that I'm afraid. *(Angrily)* I like cats. I bet the cat didn't eat Eggletina. I bet she just ran away because she hated being cooped up . . . day after day . . . week after week . . . year after year . . . Like I do! *(A sob)* . . . Oh, I know papa is a wonderful Borrower. I know we've managed to stay when all the others have gone. But what has it done for us, in the end? I don't think it's so clever to live on alone, for ever and ever, in a great, big, half-empty house, under the floor, with no one to talk to, no one to play with, nothing to see but dust and passages, no light but candlelight and firelight and what comes through the cracks. Eggletina had brothers and Eggletina had half-brothers; Eggletina had a tame mouse; Eggletina had yellow boots with jet buttons and Eggletina did get out – just once!

Maria Jones – aged 10 or 11

THE BOX OF DELIGHTS
JOHN MASEFIELD

A mysterious Punch and Judy man gives Kay Harker the magic Box of Delights, which takes him back into the days of King Arthur and beyond that to Troy. Abner Brown's gang are trying to find the magic box and they kidnap Kay's friend, little **MARIA JONES**.

In this scene the gang have released **MARIA** after questioning, and here she describes her ordeal to Kay.

Published by Heinemann Educational Books, Oxford

Maria

I don't know where I've been. I've been scrobbled just like a greenhorn.
I knew what it would be, not taking a pistol. Well, I pity them if ever I
get near them again. They won't scrobble Maria Jones a second time . . .
I was no sooner in the room than a great iron door shot up behind me
and there I was, shut in. Then rather high up on the wall an iron shutter
slid to one side and there was an iron grille with what I took to be a
lady's face; and a very silky female voice said, 'Miss Maria Jones, please
forgive any inconvenience we may have caused you in bringing you here
and, above all, don't be afraid.' 'I'm not used to being afraid,' I said;
but all the same I was afraid. 'We only brought you here,' the female
said, 'because we hope that you may be interested. We are rather in need
of a dashing young associate at the moment and we wondered whether
we might persuade you to become that.' 'Oh,' I said, 'what are you: a
gang of crooks?' 'Oh no,' she said, 'a business community.' 'Oh,' I said,
'what business does your community do?' . . . 'You would soon learn if
you would join us.' 'Why do you want me?' I asked. 'Well, you are
young,' she said, 'and full of dash. It's an interesting world for our
younger agents; lots of motor cars, lots of aeroplanes. Life is one long,
gay social whirl.' 'And what is the work?' I asked. 'Ah,' she said, 'we shall
discuss that if you expressed a willingness to become one of us.' 'If your
job was honest,' I said, 'you'd say what it is. It can't be very nice, or it
wouldn't have you in it.' 'If children are pert here,' she said, 'we make
them into dog-biscuit. Many a good watch-dog is barking now on
insolent little chits like you.' So I said, 'If ladies are pert to me I make
them into cat's-meat. Many a good caterwaul have I fed on meat like
you, cold.'

Violet Beauregarde – American

CHARLIE AND THE CHOCOLATE FACTORY
ROALD DAHL

Adapted by Richard R. George

First presented in 1973 by Richard George and the VI Grade Class of Charlotte Elementary School, New York.

Mr Willy Wonka has just re-opened his Chocolate Factory and announces in the newspapers that he has hidden five golden tickets in five Wonka Candy Bars. These could be found anywhere, in any shop, any town and in any country in the world. Whoever finds one of these tickets will have a special tour of Mr Wonka's new factory and take home enough chocolate to last them the rest of their lives. In this scene, four golden tickets have been found. The Narrator is on stage announcing the winners and inviting them to say a few words to the audience. One of these winners is **VIOLET BEAU-REGARDE**.

Published by Puffin Books, London

Violet Beauregarde

(Chewing ferociously on gum, waving arms excitedly, talking in a rapid and loud manner, from somewhere in audience) I'm a gum-chewer normally, but when I heard about these ticket things of Mr Wonka's, I laid off the gum and switched to candy bars in the hope of striking it lucky. *Now*, of course, I'm right back on gum. I just *adore* gum. I can't do without it. I munch it all day long except for a few minutes at mealtimes when I take it out and stick it behind my ear for safe-keeping. To tell you the honest truth, I simply wouldn't feel *comfortable* if I didn't have that little wedge of gum to chew on every moment of the day, I really wouldn't. My mother says it's not ladylike and it looks ugly to see a girl's jaws going up and down like mine do all the time, but I don't agree. And who's she to criticise, anyway, because if you ask me, I'd say that *her* jaws are going up and down almost as much as mine are just from *yelling* at me every minute of the day. And now, it may interest you to know that this piece of gum I'm chewing right at this moment is one I've been working on for over *three months solid*. That's a record, that is. It's beaten the record held by my best friend, Miss Cornelia Prinzmetel. And was she ever mad! It's my most treasured possession now, this piece of gum is. At nights, I just stick it on the end of the bedpost, and it's as good as ever in the mornings . . .

Perduta

DAUGHTERS OF VENICE
DON TAYLOR

First produced by the Chiswick Youth Theatre at the Waterman's Arts Centre in 1991, and then professionally by the Quercus Theatre Company at the Wilde Theatre in 1993. Set in eighteenth century Venice, the 'Daughters' of the title are the orphans taken in and cared for by the sisters of the Convent of the Pieta – famous for its choir and orchestra, the 'Coro'.

It is Carnival time and **PERDUTA**, who works with the Coro as a copyist, is sitting in the library sorting music with four other young girls. They are bored and complaining that nothing ever happens to them, when two young Italians, Pazzo and Grimaldo enter disguised, not very convincingly, as nuns.

A composite speech from Act II. Published by Samuel French, London

Perduta

Good-evening, Sisters . . . *(To* Pazzo*)* I don't think I know you, Sister. Who are you? . . . *(To the other girls)* Leave it to me. I've got an idea . . . Sisters? . . . Do you know what happened last week, Sisters? . . . Two men got in here. Actually into the convent! Terribly not allowed! . . . It was thrillingly exciting! . . . Do you know what happened? . . . They got torn to pieces. Both of them. The bits were thrown into the canal. *(The men laugh)* No, really, I'm serious! Just up that corridor, there are a thousand girls of all ages. They've only just got off to sleep. They're really tough girls, they are, from the streets of Venice, all ages, up to nineteen . . . They get very angry, those girls do, if the convent is desecrated. They fell on those two poor fellows like a pack of wolves. Didn't they girls? . . . You couldn't help feeling sorry for them . . . They were simply overwhelmed! . . . They were very brave and strong. But they didn't have a chance . . . Not against a thousand girls in a raging fury! . . . Tore them to pieces. It was terrible. We little ones had to clear up all the blood. Then some of the brawny nuns, the tough ones with big muscles, put all the bits in a basket and threw them into the canal. The Doge's secret police came here a week later, looking for them. Apparently they were criminals on the run. But they didn't find a thing. Not one shred of flesh! Not a chip of bone! Not a fingernail! Not a hair! They just disappeared. From the face of the earth. For ever and ever. Amen . . . They got caught, of course. If they'd managed to slip out without being suspected . . . *(The men run off)* And next time you want to be a nun, make sure your boots aren't showing!

Eva – German, aged 9

KINDERTRANSPORT
DIANE SAMUELS

First produced by the Soho Theatre Company at the Cockpit Theatre in 1993, and at the Vaudeville Theatre in 1996. Between 1938 and 1939 nearly ten thousand children, mostly Jewish, were sent from Germany to Britain. One of these children, EVA Schlesinger, arrives in Manchester, expecting her parents to join her later. When her parents fail to escape the holocaust she changes her name to Evelyn and begins the process of becoming an English schoolgirl.

In this scene **EVA** is at the window of a railway carriage surrounded by other refugees, waving goodbye to her mother and father as the train moves out of the station. From then on she passes through the German border and on to Holland. We see her leaning over the rail of the boat bound for England and finally disembarking at Harwich.

Published by Nick Hern Books Ltd, London

Eva

(On the train bound for England) Mutti! Vati! Hello! See. I did get into the carriage. I said I would. See, I'm not crying. I said I wouldn't. I can't open the window! It's sealed tight! Why've you taken your gloves off? You're knocking too hard. Your knuckles are going red! What? I can't hear you! *(Train noise)* Louder! Louder! What! I can't hear! I can't . . . See you in England. *(The train starts to move. EVA sits down)* I mustn't stare at that cross-eyed boy. What if he talks to me? *(A young child starts to cry)* You mustn't cry. There's no point. Stop it! . . . We'll all see our muttis and vatis soon enough . . . And don't look at that cross-eyed boy. *(The crying continues. EVA starts to sing)*

> Hoppe, hoppe Reiter/Wenn er fällt dann schreit er/
> Fällt er in den Graben/Fressen ihn die Raben
> *(Hop hop hop hop Rider/Do not fall beside her/*
> *If into the ditch you fall/The Ratman gets you all)*

(Announcing to everyone in the train) Did any of you know? In England all the men have pipes and look like Sherlock Holmes and everyone has a dog. It's the border! The border! Can't get us now! We're out! Out! Stuff your stupid Hitler!

(Sounds of train stopping. EVA is eating greedily) You know what? That Dutch lady said we can have as many cakes as we want. And sweets. And lemonade. I'm going to stuff my pockets for later. Who says it's naughty? They all want us to be happy, don't they? Well, that's what I'm doing. Making myself happy.

(Sound of ship's horn) You know what? If you lick your lips you'll taste the salt. Sea salt. What d'you mean, Hook of Holland? It can't be. It's nothing like one. It isn't. Look at it. How's that a hook? *(Coughing)* Excuse me . . . *(About to be sick)* . . . it won't come . . . No, I'm fine . . . Really . . . It's just nothing . . . Nothing will come out of me.

(Ship's horn) This is Harwich, you know. It really is England . . . *(Sounds of disembarkation)* Can you go through just like that? Don't they search you? *(She picks up a penny)* A penny. They have big money here. It must be a sign of good luck.

First Fairy

A MIDSUMMER NIGHT'S DREAM
WILLIAM SHAKESPEARE

Theatres were closed between 1593 and 1594 because of the plague, so the play was probably first performed just before or just after this period and printed in 1600.

There is trouble in Fairyland. The King and Queen of the Fairies, 'Oberon' and 'Titania', have quarrelled over the possession of a little Indian boy.

The **FAIRY** is awaiting the arrival of Titania and is met by Oberon's servant, Puck, who asks her where she is going.

PUCK: *How now. Spirit. Whither wander you?*

She tells him she serves the Fairy Queen, then recognises him as Robin Goodfellow, also known as the mischievous spirit Puck. They are interrupted by the arrival of the King and Queen.

Note: This scene between 'Puck' and the 'Fairy' can also be played as a duologue.

Penguin Drama Theatre

'orbs'	fairy rings – circles of darker grass
'pensioners'	attendants
'lob'	clown
'elves'	boy fairies
'shrewd'	mischievous
'villagery'	villages
'skim milk'	steal cream
'bootless'	fruitless
'barm'	froth on the ale
'Hobgoblin'	another name for 'Puck'

Fairy

Enter a FAIRY *at one door, and* Puck
(Robin Goodfellow) *at another*
Over hill, over dale,
　Thorough bush, thorough briar,
Over park, over pale,
　Thorough flood, thorough fire –
I do wander everywhere
Swifter than the moon's sphere,
And I serve the Fairy Queen,
To dew her orbs upon the green.
The cowslips tall her pensioners be;
In their gold coats spots you see –
　Those be rubies, fairy favours;
　In those freckles live their savours.
I must go seek some dewdrops here,
And hang a pearl in every cowslip's ear.
Farewell, thou lob of spirits; I'll be gone.
Our Queen and all her elves come here anon . . .
Either I mistake your shape and making quite,
Or else you are that shrewd and knavish sprite
Called Robin Goodfellow. Are not you he
That frights the maidens of the villagery,
Skim milk, and sometimes labour in the quern,
And bootless make the breathless housewife churn,
And sometime make the drink to bear no barm,
Mislead night-wanderers, laughing at their harm?
Those that 'Hobgoblin' call you, and 'Sweet Puck',
You do their work, and they shall have good luck.
Are not you he?

Princess Irene – young

THE PRINCESS AND THE GOBLIN

A children's play by Stuart Paterson
From the book by George MacDonald

First performed by the Dundee Repertory Company in 1993. This is the story of a kind but wayward princess, who having run away from her strict nurse is captured by Crown Prince Krankl, heir to the Goblin Kingdom.

This scene takes place in the goblin palace, deep under the mountain. **IRENE** thinks she has escaped from Krankl, but he suddenly appears, accompanied by Fannon, a small dragon. Krankl announces that he intends to marry her and that one day she will be Queen of the goblins. **IRENE** recognises Fannon as the dragon she had once helped when he hurt his wing. She begs Krankl to take the dragon away, knowing that whatever she asks he will do exactly the opposite. Left alone she approaches Fannon, who at first lets out a tremendous roar.

Irene

(To Krankle*)* Go! Please go . . . but I ask one favour – take that horrible dragon with you! . . . I hate him. He's ugly and fierce and he scares me . . . *(*Krankl *exits)* I knew if I asked for one thing, he would do the other. All cruel people are the same . . . You're a good dragon, aren't you? *(*Fannon *roars fiercely)* Don't be angry, Fannon . . . *(He roars more loudly, comes towards her menacingly)* Fannon? You do remember me, don't you? *(*Fannon *charges at her, roaring, flailing his wings)* Fannon! Stop it! Please! *(She covers her eyes in terror, but* Fannon *rushes past her and flushes out* Sly *who has been hiding)* The goblin spy! *(*Fannon *chases* Sly*)* Good boy, Fannon! Chase him! Bite his legs! Go on! *(She watches as* Fannon *chases* Sly *off)* Come back, Fannon! Don't leave me here on my own! Let him go. Please, come back. *(Enter* Fannon*)* Good dragon. I thought you had forgotten me . . . We are friends, aren't we? *(*Fannon *gives a gentle roar)* Come over here, then. Come on. *(He goes to her and she strokes and pats him)* Let me see your wing. *(She examines his wing)* It's nearly all better now. Soon you'll be able to fly. You really are the best dragon in the whole world . . . And your wings are so beautiful. Perhaps one day you will let me sit on your back and we'll fly over oceans, forests and mountains . . . But remember and pretend to be fierce! *(She roars)* *(*Fannon *licks her)* Stop licking! I'm glad I've found a friend. It's like I've been swallowed down into the belly of some huge monster . . . But you! You've been a prisoner in the dark for six years. Do you ever dream of the sun? Do you dream of a ball of fire hanging in the sky like a giant lamp? You keep dreaming, Fannon, and I'll take you out of here. I'll find a way, I promise! *(Looks off)* He's coming back! Quickly, pretend to be fierce! As fierce as you can!

Mr Fox

FANTASTIC MR FOX
ROALD DAHL

Adapted by Sally Reid

First presented in Easter Term 1987 by children and staff of St. Andrew's Primary School, Buckland, Monachorum, Devon.

Three farmers, Bean, Boggis and Bunce are determined to get rid of **MR FOX** and his young family. They have already shot off **MR FOX**'s beautiful tail and now they have brought in tractors and mechanical shovels to dig them out.

In this scene, set in a tunnel made by the foxes, Mr Badger and his young son have come to complain on behalf of all the other animals living underground, that they are unable to get out of their homes to look for food. They are blaming the foxes for their plight. But the fantastic **MR FOX** tells them he has devised a cunning plan.

Published by Penguin, London

Mr Fox

(Conspiratorially to Mr Badger*)* Do you know where we've just been?
. . . Right inside Boggis's Chicken House Number One! . . . Yes! But
that is nothing to where we are going now . . . This way, Badger, old
chap. *(Turns and points to stage right with back to* Badger*)* . . . Don't
talk about my tail, *please*. It's a painful subject. Nose down, and DIG.
*(They dig along stage towards stage right – feel imaginary floorboards
above head)* If I am not mistaken, my dear Badger *(whispering)*, we are
now underneath the farm which belongs to that nasty little pot-bellied
dwarf, Bunce. We are, in fact, directly underneath the most INTER-
ESTING part of that farm. *(Puts his head through imaginary floorboard)*
Yes, I've done it again! I've hit it smack on the nose. Right in the bull's-
eye. Come and look! *(They scramble out)* This, my dear old Badger, is
Bunce's Mighty Storehouse! All his finest stuff is stored here before he
sends it off to market. Just feast your eyes on that. What do you think
of it, eh? Pretty good grub. (Badger *and three young foxes run to grab
at food)* Stop! This is *my* party, so *I* shall do the choosing. We mustn't
overdo it. Mustn't give the game away! Mustn't let them know what
we've been up to. We must be neat and tidy and just take a few of the
choicest morsels. So, to start with we shall have four plump young ducks!
(Reaches up for four from the shelf) Oh, how lovely and fat they are.
No wonder Bunce gets a special price for them in the market. All right,
Badger, lend me a hand to get them down. You children can help as well
. . . There we go . . . Goodness me, look how your mouths are watering
. . . Gently does it . . . That's the way . . . And what about a couple of
nice smoked hams . . . I adore smoked ham, don't you, Badger? . . .
Worry me? What? . . . All this stealing? . . . *(Arm around* Mr Badger*)*
My dear old furry frump, do you know anyone in the *whole world* who
wouldn't swipe a few chickens if his children were starving to death?
(Pause as Mr Badger *thinks)* You are far too respectable.

Flibberty – a goblin

FLIBBERTY AND THE PENGUIN
DAVID WOOD

First presented at The Swan Theatre, Worcester by the Worcester Repertory Company in 1971.

A young penguin has come from Iceland to find his mother and father and meets up with **FLIBBERTY**, a friendly goblin who helps him in his search.

At the opening of the play, set in a clearing in the Forest, the penguin comes in carrying a small suitcase. He sits down underneath a tree and falls asleep. As he dozes, an acorn drops down on his head and wakes him up. Then another and another. He looks up to see **FLIBBERTY** sitting up in the branches laughing down at him. **FLIBBERTY** talks to the penguin who is unable to answer, but tries to make him understand, and invites the audience to help him.

Published by Samuel French, London

Flibberty

Hallo!
The Penguin *does not answer, but sadly rubs the top of his head*
I didn't hurt you, did I? They're only acorns.
The Penguin *nods as* FLIBBERTY *jumps down from the tree and comes up to him*
I'm sorry. Look, I'm Flibberty.
The Penguin *puts his head on one side enquiringly*
Flibberty. Well, Flibberty Gibbet, really, but that's too long for anyone to remember, so everyone calls me Flibberty. I'm a goblin. What are you?
The Penguin *points to himself, but makes no reply*
Yes, but what are you?
The Penguin *shrugs his shoulders, points to his beak, and shakes his head*
What's the matter? Can't you speak?
The Penguin *shakes his head*
Oh dear! You poor thing. That must make life very difficult for you. I mean, I don't even know what you are. I've never seen anything like . . .
(Noticing the audience, he speaks to them) You don't know what he is, do you?

Audience participation
A what? A Penguin? *(To the* Penguin*)* Is that right?
The Penguin *nods*
Where have you come from?
The Penguin *mimes being very cold, slapping himself to keep warm*
(To the audience) What's he saying? He looks cold, doesn't he? Where?
Iceland? *(To the* Penguin*)* Is that right?
The Penguin nods
(To the audience) Oh, well done! *(To the* Penguin*)* How did you get from
Iceland all the way here?
The Penguin *mimes 'walking'. The audience shout this out*
You walked?
The Penguin *nods, then mimes 'swimming'*
And swam across the sea?
The Penguin *nods, then mimes 'climbing mountains'*
And climbed mountains? My, no wonder you look tired. But why have
you come here, to this forest?
The Penguin *mimes 'searching for someone'*
Looking for someone?
The Penguin *mimes 'not one person, two people'*
Two people. *(To the audience)* Who could they be?
The Penguin *opens his case and takes out a photo of his father and
mother*
Who are they? *(Helped by the audience)* Your mother and father?
The Penguin *nods*
Well, where are they?
The Penguin *shrugs his shoulders*
Where? Oh, you don't know. Of course, that's why you're looking for
them. What happened to them?
The Penguin *mimes 'I don't know, they just disappeared'*
What? They disappeared?
The Penguin *nods and begins to sob*
And you've come all this way to find them?
The Penguin *nods, sobbing*
Oh! *(To the audience)* Well, I think we ought to help him, don't you?
(To Penguin*)* Come on, let's start looking for your father and mother.

James

JAMES AND THE GIANT PEACH
ROALD DAHL

Adapted by Richard R. George

Written in 1961 and adapted as a play in 1982 by American school teacher, Richard George.

JAMES has escaped from his dreadful guardians, Aunt Spiker and Aunt Sponge, and sets off inside the Giant Peach on his amazing adventures. He is accompanied by his friends, Earthworm, Centipede, Old-Green-Grasshopper, Spider, Ladybird and Glow-Worm.

In this scene, the Peach has broken through the garden fence, rolled down the hill and on and on towards Dover, where it hurtles over the white cliffs and into the sea. Now it is floating further and further out, bobbing along on the waves. **JAMES** and his friends have climbed out and are sitting on top of it, when the Centipede looks towards the horizon and sees a thin black thing moving towards them. It is a shark. Soon there are more sharks and they begin to attack the Peach. Ladybird appeals to **JAMES**. Surely he can think of something before they are all eaten alive.

Published by Penguin, London

James

There *is* something that I believe we might try. I'm not saying it'll work
. . . I . . . I . . . I'm afraid it's no good . . . after all . . . *(Shaking his
head)* I'm terribly sorry. I forgot. We don't have any string. We'd need
hundreds of yards of string to make this work . . . The Silkworm? You
can wake him up and make him spin? And you, Spider, can spin just as
well as any Silkworm! Can you make enough between you? And would
it be strong? . . . I'm going to lift this Peach clear out of the water! With
seagulls! The place is full of them. Look up there! *(Pointing towards the
sky)* I'm going to take a long silk string and I'm going to loop one end
of it around a seagull's neck. And then I'm going to tie the other end
to the stem of the Peach. (JAMES *points to the* Peach *stem, which is
standing up like a mast in the middle of the stage)* Then I'm going to
get another seagull and do the same thing again, and then another and
another . . . there's no shortage of seagulls. Look for yourself. We'll probably need four hundred, five hundred . . . maybe even a thousand . . .
I don't know . . . I shall simply go on hooking them up to the stem
until we have enough to lift us. It's like balloons. You give someone
enough balloons to hold, I mean *really* enough, then up he goes. And a
seagull has far more lifting power than a balloon. If only we have *time*
to do it . . . We'll do it with bait. With a worm, of course. Seagulls love
worms, didn't you know that? And luckily for us, we have here the
biggest, fattest, juciest Earthworm . . . The seagulls have already spotted
him. That's why there are so many of them circling around. But they
daren't come down and get him while all the rest of us are standing here.
So this is what we'll do . . . *(He puts his arm around* Earthworm) I won't
let them *touch* you. I promise I won't! But we've got to hurry! Look down
there! Action stations! There's not a moment to lose! All hands below
deck except Earthworm!

Edmund

THE LION, THE WITCH AND THE WARDROBE
C.S. LEWIS

Dramatised by Adrian Mitchell

First performed in 1998 at the Royal Shakespeare Theatre, Stratford-upon-Avon and transferred to the Barbican Theatre, London in 1999.

This is the story of four children, Lucy, Susan, Peter and **EDMUND**, who are evacuated to the country during the London Blitz. Exploring the attic in their new home they discover an old wardrobe – the gateway opening out into the Land of Narnia. Narnia is under a spell, and the four children soon find themselves caught up in an adventure that leads to a final struggle between the powers of good and evil – the Lion, Aslan and the wicked White Witch. **EDMUND** is the first to meet the White Witch. She wraps him in her fur mantle, feeds him Turkish Delight and makes him promise to bring the other children to see her.

This scene is set in the courtyard of the Witch's house at night. **EDMUND** enters cautiously. There are shadowy figures of people and animals all around him – standing very still. He cowers away from an enormous lion, crouched and ready to spring, then realises it is only a statue – the statue of the great Aslan.

Published by Oberon Books, London

Edmund

A lion! [EDMUND *cowers away from an enormous lion crouched as if it is ready to spring*] Why's it standing so still? *(He ventures a little nearer)* Hey, its head's all covered in snow. Only a statue. *(He walks forward and touches the lion's head, very quickly)* Cold stone! So this is the great Lion Aslan! The Queen's turned him into stone. So that's the end of all their fine ideas! *(He takes a stub of pencil out of his pocket and scribbles a moustache and spectacles on the lion's head)* Who's afraid of Aslan? Yah! Stupid old Aslan! How do you like being a statue? [EDMUND *moves on across the courtyard among stone statues of satyrs, wolves, bears, foxes and cat-a-mountains and dryads and a centaur and a winged horse and a dragon. Right in the middle stands a stone giant.* EDMUND *moves past the giant gingerly towards stone steps leading to a doorway from which a pale light shines. Across the threshold lies a great wolf]* It's all right – only a stone wolf. It couldn't hurt a flea.

(But as EDMUND *raises his leg to step over the wolf, the huge creature rises and opens its mouth and speaks in a growling voice. It is* Maugrim *the wolf, head of the Witch's Secret Police)*

(Trembling) If you please, sir. My name is Edmund, and I'm the Son of Adam Her Majesty met in the wood the other day and I've come to bring her the news that my brother and sisters are now in Narnia – quite close, at the Beavers' house. She – she wanted to see them. Who are you, sir? . . . [Maugrim: *I am Maugrim, the Chief of the Queen's Secret Police]* . . . Will you tell Her Majesty I am here? . . . [Maugrim *vanishes into the house.* EDMUND *stands very still]* It's hard to stand still when you're trembling. I mustn't be afraid. Try to think about something nice . . . ah, yes . . . Turkish Delight . . . Turkish Delight . . . [Maugrim *comes bounding out of the house and escorts* EDMUND *in through the stone doorway. On the throne, lit by a single lamp, sits the* Witch. Maugrim *escorts* EDMUND *towards her.* EDMUND *bows to the* Witch] *(Eagerly)* I've come, your Majesty . . . Please, your Majesty, I've done the best I can. They're in Mr and Mrs Beaver's house . . . The Beaver says – Aslan is on the move . . . They're going to meet him at the Stone Table . . . that's what the Beaver said . . . Please, your Majesty, I didn't have much lunch. Could I have some Turkish Delight?

Peter – aged 10

THE RAILWAY CHILDREN
E. NESBIT

First published in 1906 and more than fifty years later made into a BBC Children's Television series – and finally a feature film.

Three children, Bobbie, **PETER** and Phyllis, lived happily in their comfortable London house, until one day some men came and took away their father. Their Mother was left with very little money and they were forced to go and live in a not very nice house in the country. A railway line ran nearby, and in those days there were lots of things to do beside a railway. All sorts of people travelled by train – and 'the Railway Children' made friends with some of them.

They find a young boy lying in the tunnel with a broken leg and run for help. They bring him home and their mother puts him to bed and calls the doctor. In this scene they are waiting downstairs in the parlour, listening to the sounds of the doctor overhead and the groans of his patient. The girls are very distressed, but **PETER** finds it all very exciting. He teases the girls, and despite their protests suggests a game of bone-setting. This gives Bobbie and Phyllis their opportunity for revenge.

Published by Penguin Books, London

Peter

It *is* horrible, but it's very exciting. I wish doctors weren't so stuck up about who'll they'll have in the room when they're doing things. I should most awfully like to see a leg set. I believe the bones crunch like anything . . . How are you going to be Red Cross Nurses, like you were talking of coming home, if you can't even stand hearing me say about bones crunching? You'd have to *hear* them crunch on the field of battle – and be steeped in gore up to the elbows . . . It would be a jolly good thing for you if I were to talk to you every day for half an hour about broken bones and people's insides, so as to get you used to it . . . I'll tell you what they do, they strap the broken man down so that he can't resist or interfere with their doctorish designs, and then someone holds his head, and someone holds his leg – the broken one, and pulls it till the bones fit in – with a crunch, mind you! Then they strap it up and – let's play at bone-setting! . . . I'll get the splints and bandages, you get the couch of suffering ready. *(He fetches ropes and two boards for splints)* Now, then. *(He lies down on the settle, groaning most grievously)* Not so tight. You'll break my other leg . . . That's enough, I can't move at all. Oh my poor leg! . . . Shall we play it's bleeding freely . . . *(The girls move away leaving* PETER *tied up)* . . . You beasts! *(He tries to free himself)* I'll yell, and Mother will come!

Eustace

THE VOYAGE OF THE DAWN TREADER
C.S. LEWIS

Adapted for the stage by Glyn Robbins
First performed at the Theatre Royal, Bath in 1986

The *Dawn Treader* is a dragon-ship, captained by Caspian, the young King of Narnia. He has sworn an oath to search out the seven missing Lords who were sent out on a dangerous mission across the sea beyond the Eastern Ocean and have never returned.

He is joined by his friends, Lucy, Edmund and their cousin, **EUSTACE**, and Reepicheap – the most valiant mouse in the world.

In this scene they find themselves shipwrecked on Dragon-Island. **EUSTACE** is cross and has left the others and wandered off into a cave. They come looking for him but he is nowhere to be seen. Their ship has been repaired and they are ready to sail again. As they head towards the cave a dragon roars. They run and hide, but Reepicheap prepares to fight. A dragon appears out of the cave limping. Tears are running down its face. They ask if it is human and it nods. Is it by any chance, Edmund? The dragon nods again violently.

They're not sure what to do. They can't leave Edmund, but how do you feed a dragon? They are extremely tired now and decide to settle down to sleep whilst the 'dragon' goes back into the cave.

In the following silence the silhouette of a dragon flies across the face of the moon, and we hear the terrible roar of a lion. Everyone takes up defensive positions. They hear footsteps and **EUSTACE** enters.

In this scene **EUSTACE** describes what happened to him.

Samuel French, London

Eustace

EUSTACE *enters*

Are you there, Reep? (Reepicheep *Is that really you, Eustace?*) Yes, Reep, I'm back. Back as myself . . . (Lucy *Tell us what happened, Eustace.*) Well, I was lying in the cave, in terrible pain, trying to sleep thinking about what Reep had told me. Then I saw this huge lion coming towards me . . . I was terribly afraid – especially when it told me to follow it . . . (Reepicheep *You mean the lion spoke to you?*) No, I don't think he did. But he told me somehow, all the same. And I followed him a long way into the mountains to a sort of well of cool water. I knew that if I could only get into the water it would ease the pain in my leg. But the lion told me to get undressed first. So I tried to scratch myself, and first my dragon scales fell off, then my skin – just like peeling a banana. It was lovely, all the pain had gone. I was just going to step into the water, when I looked down and found the scales had all come back. I scratched off three sets of scales. Then the lion said – or told me somehow: 'You will have to let *me* undress you'. The first tear he made was so deep that I thought it had gone right into my heart. That's when I screamed. Well, he peeled it all off, picked me up, and threw me into the water. It stung like anything at first, but then all the pain went away and I had turned into a boy again. It was all like a bad dream. With a happy ending.

Lucy

INVISIBLE FRIENDS
ALAN AYCKBOURN

First performed in 1989 at the Stephen Joseph Theatre, Scarborough, the play is about a very ordinary girl called **LUCY**. With her father glued to the telly, her mother preoccupied with local gossip and her brother, known as 'Grisly Gary', shut up in his room listening to heavy metal music, no one wants to know about her place in the school swimming team. So **LUCY** revives her childhood fantasy friend, Zara. Only this time, Zara materialises, bringing with her an idealised father and brother, and showing her how to make her real family vanish.

In this scene, **LUCY** has just come out of Gary's bedroom having failed to make him listen to her, as she tries to tell him her good news above the sound of the stereo. She enters her own room and introduces the audience to her invisible friend, Zara.

Published by Faber & Faber, London

Lucy

You may have heard my mum talking about my invisible friend. Do you remember? Well, that's my invisible friend, Zara. *(Introducing her)* This is Zara. I want you to meet Zara. Zara, say hallo. That's it. Will you say hallo to Zara, my invisible friend? I invented Zara – oh, years ago – when I was seven or eight. Just for fun. I think I was ill at that time and wasn't allowed to play with any of my real friends, so I made up Zara. She's my special friend that no one can see except me. Of course, I can't really see her either. Not really. Although sometimes I . . . It's almost as if I could see her, sometimes. If I concentrate very hard it's like I can just glimpse her out of the corner of my eye. *(She is thoughtful for a second)* Still. Anyway. I've kept Zara for years and years. Until they all started saying I was much too old for that sort of thing and got worried and started talking about sending for a doctor. So then I didn't take her round with me quite so much after that. But she's still here. And when I feel really sad and depressed like I do today, then I sit and talk to Zara. Zara always understands. Zara always listens. She's special. Aren't you, Zara? *(She listens to Zara)* What's that? Yes, I wish he'd turn his music down, too. I've asked him, haven't I? *(Mimicking Gary)* 'How can I hear it if I turn it down, I can't hear the bass then, can I?' I used to have pictures in here but every time he put a disc on they fell off the walls. *(Pause. The music continues)* I mean, don't get me wrong. We like loud music, don't we, Zara? We love loud music. Sometimes. *(Yelling)* BUT NOT ALL THE TIME.
(Pause)
Why doesn't he ever listen to quiet music? Just once. Wouldn't that be nice? . . . But if he did that, he wouldn't be Grisly Gary then, would he?
(Pause)
Oh, Zara, did I tell you I've been picked for the school swimming team? Isn't that exciting? Yes. Thank you. I'm glad you're excited, too. Good.
(Pause)
(Shouting) IF ANYONE IS INTERESTED AT ALL, I WAS PICKED FOR THE SCHOOL SWIMMING TEAM TODAY. WHAT ABOUT THAT, FOLKS?
(She listens. No reply)
Great. Thanks for your support, everyone. *(Tearful)* They might at least . . . They could have at least . . . Oh, Zara . . . I know you're always here, but sometimes I get so . . . lonely . . .
(She sits on her bed, sad, angry and frustrated)

Suzy

MR A'S AMAZING MAZE PLAYS
ALAN AYCKBOURN

First performed at the Stephen Joseph Theatre in the Round, Scarborough in 1988.

SUZY lives in a small cottage with her mother and her dog, Neville – her father went up in a hot air balloon one day and never came back down. Except for missing **SUZY**'s father they are all quite happy, until the suave Mr Accousticus moves into the mysterious old house across from their cottage and sweeps Mother off her feet.

Mr Accousticus hates noise, and since his arrival Neville has lost his bark and their friend and neighbour, Mr Passerby, has lost his operatic voice.

While Mr Accousticus is having supper with Mother, **SUZY** and Neville plan to get into his house and search for Neville's bark and Mr Passerby's operatic voice. They creep through the garden and along the path till they reach the big front door. Neville pushes it open and they find themselves in a dark hallway. At this point in the play it is up to the audience to choose which course **SUZY** and Neville should take, and the search sequence begins.

In this scene **SUZY** and Neville have found their way into Mr Accousticus's Music Room. From there they progress to the Dining Room and then on into the Conservatory.

Published by Faber & Faber, London

Suzy

[SUZY *and* Neville *enter the Music Room]* This must be the music room. Look, a piano. *(She tries a few notes)* Well, I think it's a piano. Here's a harp. *(She tries a few notes –* Neville *finds a tin whistle)* What have you got there? A whistle? *(*Neville *tries to blow it)* Sshh! Let's try that door. It's the only way out of here. *(She tries it, but it is locked)* What's this say? *(She reads something on the door)* 'I won't let you in to dine. Eat my food or drink my wine/Taste my breakfast, sip my tea/'Til you've sung a song for me.' Oh, terrific! Does that mean we have to sing to open the door? I suppose it does. You can't sing, can you, Neville, poor old thing. Wait a minute. I can't think of any songs. I know – what about the one that Mr Passerby always used to sing . . . ?

(She sings) Early one morning . . .
Just as the sun was rising . . . that's it . . .
(SUZY *has difficulty in remembering the words)*
I heard a maiden singing in the valley below.
Oh, don't deceive me,
Oh, never leave me,
How could you treat a poor maiden so?

(At the end of all this the door opens) Look, Neville, it worked! Come on, then. Dinner is served. (SUZY *and* Neville *enter the Dining Room)* I wouldn't like to eat in here very much. Not on my own. And it's so dusty. You'd get mouthfuls of fluff. *(They examine things on the table)* Ugggh! Well, it doesn't look as if anyone's even been in here for years, let alone eaten in here. On we go then. We could try those windows. They seem to open and lead to somewhere. Yes, it's full of huge plants out there. It's like a jungle. I think it's what they call a conservatory. Shall we go out there, Neville? It looks rather dangerous . . . What have you found, then? Oh, yes. It's a little concealed door. It's painted like the wall so you hardly notice it. Oh dear. Another choice. Which way shall we go then? Through this door? . . . Or through the French windows and into the jungle? . . . (SUZY *and* Neville *step out through the windows and into the conservatory)* I hope there aren't any wild animals in here . . . Like tigers. Or snakes. I don't like snakes at all. It is very thick, the undergrowth, though. You can hardly see where you're going. Neville? . . . (Neville *has somehow lost sight of* SUZY. *And now* SUZY *has lost* Neville) Neville? Don't be silly, Neville. Don't play games. We haven't got time for that. If Mr Accousticus comes back while we're here, we're in real trouble. Neville . . . Neville? *(They prowl about for a bit. Then* Neville *leaps out at* SUZY, *mistaking her for someone else. They roll about)* Neville, stop it! It's me! It's me! Neville! (Neville *stops attacking her)* Don't ever do that again. I thought you were a tiger . . . Now, how do we get out of here? If we ever do get out. What's that in the corner over there? It looks like a door . . . *(She moves over to it)* Yes, look, Neville. It's the door to a lift. Come on, let's try the lift . . .

Mary Mooney

ONCE A CATHOLIC
MARY O'MALLEY

First performed at the Royal Court Theatre in 1977 and set in the convent of Our Lady of Fatima – a Grammar School for Girls – and in and around the streets of Willesden and Harlesden, London NW10, from September 1956 to July 1957.

MARY MOONEY is a fifth former, plain and rather scruffy but with a good singing voice. Her ambition is to become a nun.

In this scene she is walking down the street with Mary McGinty and Mary Gallaher. All three are carrying satchels and eating Mars Bars. Mary McGinty has refused to wear her hat and if a prefect sees her she'll get reported. McGinty doesn't care. It wouldn't worry her if she got expelled. She wonders what she'd have to do to get expelled from 'that old dump' . . . **MARY MOONEY** is shocked. McGinty mustn't say things like that.

(McGINTY: *'Why not? Do you think a thunderbolt is gonna come hurtling down from Heaven?'*)

Amber Lane Press, Charlbury, Oxfordshire

Mary Mooney

You mustn't say things like that . . . It doesn't happen straight away. It happens when you're least expecting it. You'd better make an Act of Contrition . . . My Dad knows this man who used to be a monk. But he couldn't keep his vows so he asked if he could be released. On the day he left he came skipping down the path with his collar in his hand. And when he opened the monastery gate he saw an alsatian sitting outside. So he hung his collar around the alsatian's neck and went on his way laughing all along the road. After that he started going into pubs every night and boasting to all the people about what he'd gone and done with his collar. Then one day he went and got married. And while he was on his honeymoon he started to get a really bad pain in his back. He was in such a terrible agony he could only walk about with a stoop. And after a while he was completely bent up double. Then he started to lose his voice. He went to loads of different doctors but none of them could do anything to help him. And now he can only get about on all fours. And when he opens his mouth to say anything he barks just like a dog. Of course it's true. He lives in Shepherd's Bush . . . I bet if you were knocked down by a trolley bus this evening you'd be yelling your head off for a priest.

Angela – Manchester, aged 11–12

SIX PRIMROSES EACH
ELLEN DRYDEN

Presented by the Chiswick Youth Theatre in workshop and performance between 1985 and 1991, and set in a Church Hall in the
country during World War II (1940).

In this opening scene a group of children are waiting around in
the Church Hall. They have been evacuated from the East End of
London because of the bombing and are about to be allocated to
various homes near by. They are homesick and apprehensive but are
trying to make the best of things. **ANGELA**, a bouncy north country
girl, comes in with her side-kick, Janet. She is not an evacuee like
the others, and is staying with her Auntie in the country until the air
raids are over in Manchester. She is most unwelcoming.

From: *Six Primroses Each and Other Plays for Young Actors*

Published by First Writes Publications, London

Angela

Oh, hello! I didn't know there was anybody in here! *(Of course she did. That's why she's come in)* They must have forgotten about you . . . *(She looks them up and down)* I don't think you ought to sit on the chairs. Not till you've been disinfected! . . . No! I'm not an *evacuee*! I'm here with my Auntie Joan to pick out a couple of you. She's in there talking to Miss Deacon. They probably put you in here 'cos they think you've got nits. Or fleas. *(Janet giggles)* Or ringworm or something like that! . . . It's something dirty people get. Your hair all comes out in little round patches. A lot of the scruffy lot from London get it. They paint your head purple . . . I expect they're saving you for Mrs Fitz-Hughes at the Manor. She always takes a load of scruffy ones. They never stay long though! She's got a row of little camp beds in the stables and she makes the evacuees do all the work. Scrub the floors, clean out the pigsties, muck out the hens and black-lead all the grates. And if she has Catholics she makes them eat meat on Fridays, and she made David Goldberg eat a pig's brains – and he was sick all over and she sent him back. And she gives you bread and milk all the time. With stale bread, and she waters the milk. And no sugar. And the Major – that's her husband – he's too old to be a proper soldier – he lets us go on nature walks on his land. And he said we could pick primroses. *'The children can pick six each with one leaf, and the Teachers can pick twelve with two leaves.'* And it's freezing . . . And you have to go to church on Sunday. Or Chapel . . . It's dead funny in Chapel. My Auntie Joan goes. And the man next door hates the Chapel, and he killed his pig on a Sunday morning! We were just singing the first hymn when it started squealing its head off 'cos it knew what he was going to do, and he chased it all round the garden and it squealed and squealed and then it was quiet – and everybody looked at each other 'cos they knew he'd cut its throat and it was bleeding to death . . . *(A voice is heard from outside)* Oh that's my Auntie Joan! Come on, Janet. Well, I shouldn't think I'll see you lot again. *(With pride)* And it just so happens that Manchester is a very important industrial city, – with Docks and the Ship Canal. It's just as important as rotten old London!

Lucy – aged about 12

THE VOYAGE OF THE DAWN TREADER
C.S. LEWIS

Adapted by Glyn Robbins

First performed at the Theatre Royal, Bath in 1986, it has now been made into a feature film.

The Dawn Treader is a dragon-ship led by Caspian, the young King of Narnia, who has sworn to find the seven missing Lords, sent on a mission across the sea beyond the Eastern Ocean. On board are **LUCY**, Edmund and their cousin, Eustace.

The expedition has reached the Island of Silence ruled by a great Magician and inhabited by the invisible Thumpers. **LUCY** overhears the Thumpers planning to capture them. They are under a spell that can only be broken by a little girl – but it has to be done of her own free will. They are heavily armed and so **LUCY** agrees to help them.

In this scene she is upstairs in the Magician's house in a room lined with books. There is one huge book lying on a lectern. **LUCY** speaks aloud as she begins to turn the pages.

Published by Samuel French, London

Lucy

What a beautiful book. Without doubt the most beautiful book I have ever seen. What have we here? Spells, of course. Here's a cure for warts. Wash in a silver basin by moonlight . . . Well, I haven't got any warts, so that's no good. Here's one for toothache, and one for cramp, and another for lifting a swarm of bees. Fascinating. This one's for finding buried treasure, and here's another for remembering forgotten things – that could be really useful. Here's how to raise a wind, or fog, or rain, snow, hail or ice. My word, that's a very beautiful page. What does it say? 'A spell to make her that utters it beautiful beyond the lot of mortals.' Just think of that. To be the most beautiful woman on earth. Why princes and kings would come to ask for my hand in marriage; they would fight tournaments and mock battles for my favours; then perhaps the battles would become real ones and nation would fight nation for the honour of having me as queen and then Narnia would be laid waste together with all the lands around it. But that wouldn't matter, as long as every woman was jealous of my beauty and my power, and every man worshipped me but hopelessly, and oh! I will say that spell. I must say that spell.

(The page of the book becomes a picture of Aslan. The picture roars in anger, LUCY is very frightend and turns over the page quickly)

That was silly of me. I nearly got carried away. What's this next one? A spell that lets you know what your friends really say about you. That could be interesting. I'll say it quickily. *(She mumbles to herself)*

(The sound of a railway train)

How strange. That's a train. And that's a compartment, and there are my two schoolfriends. Marjorie Preston and Anne Featherstone.

(The page of the book becomes a picture of two girls sitting in a railway compartment . . .)

LUCY *(shouting)* Majorie Preston, you two-faced beast.

(The picture fades, and LUCY turns the page)

Well, I thought she was a lot nicer than that. I wonder if all my friends are the same. I don't want to know, really . . . Now what's this? A page with no pictures. Just some writing. What does it say? 'A spell to make hidden things visible.' That's it! That's the one I've been looking for.

Mildred Hubble – aged 11

THE WORST WITCH

Adapted by Paul Todd from Jill Murphy's books

The Worst Witch series of books, the first of which was published in 1975, toured nationally as a musical with book, music and lyrics by Paul Todd with Jill Murphy in 1991/2, and was made into a children's series for Carlton TV.

   MILDRED HUBBLE is 'The Worst Witch' at Miss Cackle's Academy for Witches – she always gets things wrong. But she manages to get by until Ethel, the teacher's pet, becomes her deadly enemy. In this scene **MILDRED** has been summoned to Miss Cackle's office to explain a recent incident. She is very nervous and hoping desperately that she won't be expelled.

Published by Puffin Books, London

Mildred

Mildred Headle, Hubmistress. I mean Hubble, Headmistress. Mildred Hubble . . . Like 'trouble', Miss, yes. Unfortunately . . . Except there's no 'o' in it . . . But there are two 'b's . . And an 'h' instead of 't', 'r'. Obviously. *(Pause)* You can borrow my pen, Miss, if yours has run out . . . Why am I here? Now, that's a very good question. I've not done anything wrong . . . much. At all, really. It's a lot of fuss about nothing, if you ask me . . . Didn't you? Oh, I'm sorry. *(She giggles nervously)* I am taking it seriously, Miss Cackle. Very, very seriously *(She giggles again)*. Sorry. It was Miss Hardbroom. And a Spelling mistake, that's all. A silly, little Spelling mistake in Miss Hardbroom's class . . . I turned Ethel into a pig. That was the mistake. It was meant to be a frog. I've got to have extra lessons. They're really, really complicated, all the animal spells, aren't they? . . . Right. Well, it all started when I was given a tabby instead of a black cat – I mean, everyone else got a black cat and H.B. – I mean, Miss Hardbroom – probably did it on purpose, but Tabby's lovely and really intelligent and things, but Ethel made fun of him and I didn't like it 'cos he can't answer back, and Ethel said that we were both as bad as each other (but she didn't say what at!) so I said: 'You'd better be quiet' and she said 'Won't!' and I said 'If you don't, I'll –' and she said 'What?' and I said I'd turn her into a frog and she said I could-n't 'cos I didn't know the spell. So I did. Well, I didn't. I nearly did. But I've changed her back. She's a bit disgruntled but she's alright. Apart from the occasional oink . . . Witches' Code, Rule Number Seven Paragraph Two . . . ? *(Pause)* No, I'm afraid that escapes me at present . . . 'It is not customary . . . '? Oh, yes! 'It is not customary to practise tricks on your fellows' . . . No, Miss, I won't forget in future . . . Can I? Really? I can go? I thought I was going to be – *(Pause)* You're right. The extra lessons with H.B. – Hardbroom'll be punishment enough. Thank you, Miss Cackle. *(She starts to exit, then turns)* When you were little? Extra Chanting lessons? Really? *(Pause)* For two whole terms? *(Pause)* I won't tell a soul. Honestly. Not a word. Goodbye, Miss Cackle. And thank you. I'll see you soon. *(Re-considering)* I didn't mean that. At least, I hope I didn't. *(Moving off, to herself)* Well, well, well . . . who would've thought Miss Cackle was ever a little girl . . .?

Marcus – aged 12–13

THE CHILDREN'S WARD
ELLEN DRYDEN

Presented by the Chiswick Youth Theatre in workshop and performance between 1985 and 1991, this award-winning short play is set in the children's ward of a large modern hospital.

MARCUS is a lively, energetic long-stay patient. His mother and little brother have come to visit him in the Playroom, but he has retreated back into the ward to get away from them. He sits on his bed talking to two other patients: Chris, who is building a model village which MARCUS's brother has been 'mucking about with', and Patrick, who has just been admitted with suspected appendicitis.

From: *Six Primroses Each and Other Plays for Young Actors*

Published by First Writes Publications, London

Marcus

'Lo Chris . . . *(He goes and sits on his bed which is immediately opposite
Patrick's)* My little brother's here. He's in the Playroom. That's why I
came in here. He's screaming the place down. He wants the little house,
he says. My Mum keeps shovelling him into the Wendy House and he
keeps kicking the other kids. I wish she wouldn't keep bringing him . . .
She spoils him rotten. I tell her not to bring him but she thinks he might
get what I've got so she wants him to get used to Hospital . . . There's
some horrible kids in this place but he's worse than any of them. My
Mum doesn't believe in violence so she never hits him – she goes berserk
when I do. And she sits up all night with my Dad discussing my aggressive tendencies and where she's gone wrong. *(He chuckles delightedly)*
She goes to consciousness raising groups . . . She's going veggie as well.
She cooks these great big panfuls of beans and stuff. Looks like puke.
She reckons it's diet why I'm in here. My Dad stops off at Macdonald's
on the way home from work and says he's not too hungry when he gets
in. So she saves up all the bean stuff and puts some lentils in it and
gives it him the next day. Do you know, she won't let me and my brother
have any aggressive toys or anything . . . She's trying to find a Save the
Whale game for my computer. I can't have nasty War games 'cos she's
trying to breed a better sort of boy . . . My brother's the most violent
little devil ever. I hate him. He got chucked out of his playgroup last
week . . . He set fire to the Wendy House.

Ernie

ERNIE'S INCREDIBLE ILLUCINATIONS
ALAN AYCKBOURN

First published in 1969 and set in a doctor's surgery and wherever **ERNIE**'s imagination takes him.

    ERNIE's Mum and Dad are worried about what they call his 'illucinations' – so worried that they take him to the Doctor. They explain that not only are they concerned for **ERNIE**, but also for themselves, as he seems to be drawing *them* into his imaginings as well. The Doctor refuses to take this seriously until he too is forced to take part in one of **ERNIE**'s incredible 'illucinations'.

    In this scene, **ERNIE** explains to the Doctor how he managed to involve his Mum and his Auntie May in his 'illucinations', acting out scenes where his home is invaded by soldiers and his Auntie takes part in the world heavyweight boxing contest against 'The Kid'.

Published by Faber & Faber, London

Ernie

It started with these daydreams. You know, the sort everybody gets. Where you suddenly score a hat trick in the first five minutes of the Cup Final, or you bowl out the West Indies for ten runs – or saving your granny from a blazing helicopter, all that sort of rubbish. It was one wet Saturday afternoon and me and my mum and dad were all sitting about in the happy home having one of those exciting afternoon rave-ups we usually have in our house. [ERNIE *sits in the* Doctor's *chair and starts to read a book]* Meanwhile – I was reading a book about the French wartime resistance workers and of the dangers they faced – often arrested in their homes. I started wondering what would happen if a squad of soldiers turned up at our front door, having been tipped off about the secret radio transmitter hidden in our cistern – when suddenly . . . I shouldn't go out there, Mum . . . I said don't go out there . . . It's not the milkman. It's a squad of enemy soldiers . . . They've come for me . . . They've found out about the radio transmitter . . . *[The soldiers charge the door. A loud crash]* Don't go out, Mum . . . Don't go! . . . Mum . . . [ERNIE *stepping forward]* Well, Mum and Dad decided that the best thing to do was to pretend it hadn't happened. That was usually the way they coped with all emergencies . . . And then – Auntie May arrived to stay. I liked my Auntie May. (Auntie May *enters)* . . . And Auntie May took me to the fair . . . Oh, come on Auntie. Let's go in and watch the boxing . . . This way, Auntie . . . Auntie, where are you going? . . . Auntie! [ERNIE *stepping forward]* And then suddenly I got this idea. Maybe Auntie May could be the new heavyweight champion of the world . . . *[The bell rings and* Auntie May *comes bouncing out of her corner – she bombards* The Kid *with punches.* ERNIE, *commentator style]* And Auntie May moves in again and catches The Kid with a left and a right to the body and there's a right-cross to the head – and that really hurt him – and it looks from here as if the champ is in real trouble . . . as this amazing sixty-eight-year-old challenger follows up with a series of sharp left-jabs – one, two, three, four jabs . . . (The Kid *is reeling]* And then, bang, a right-hook and he's down . . . ! [The Kid *goes down on his knees. The crowd cheers* . . . The Kid *gets up again]* And The Kid's on his feet but he's no idea where he is – and there's that tremendous right upper-cut – and he's down again! . . .

Albert – very young

IN SERVICE
ELLEN DRYDEN

Presented by the Chiswick Youth Theatre in workshop and performance between 1985 and 1991, this short play is set in the attic and kitchen of a large Victorian house and depicts a day in the life of young people in service in the 1890s.

It is dawn and two of the maids are already at work in the scullery, when a third maid, Emily, brings in **ALBERT** – a small, wiry, impudent-looking boy – barefoot and covered in mud. She explains that he is a mudlark, found by the Young Lady of the house, who has 'a lot of silly ideas about looking after the poor'. Lavinia, a young nursery maid from the country, is handed a bucket and brush and ordered to clean up **ALBERT**. As she does so, he begins to tell her about his life as a mudlark.

From: *Six Primroses Each and Other Plays for Young Actors*

Published by First Writes Publications, London

Albert

You go in up to your knees this weather. I bin in up to me waist. I likes to nip in between the barges as well. That's where you get the best stuff. That's where you get the pitch all over you. Off of the barges . . . the pitch . . . off the bottoms. *(He looks interestedly at his arm)* That's horse muck from the stables that is! . . . In the House of Correction they stood you in the yard and hosed you down. Knocked you off your feet that did . . . Been there four times. I prigged some coal from the barges and they got me. I was looking for copper nails. They're the best but there wasn't none. Prison's all right in the winter. They give you shoes and a shirt. It's powerful hard on the feet in the winter. With the ice . . . And the broken glass. That's bad . . . There look. A broken bottle done that. Sliced through them toes. Still. If you ain't got no toes you can't get no chilblains . . . The mud blocked up the ends and I don't miss them toes now . . . I live back of King James Stairs. Down Wapping Wall. My mum sells fish down there. When she can. But she's been in the Fever Hospital a long time now. My Dad fell between the barges. Broke his back. Drunk as usual. So me and our Nellie went mudlarking. *(Proudly)* I get fourpence a day . . . you can on a good day . . . If I could find a hammer or a saw I could get eightpence then we'd be all right. Will she – the Lady – will she, do you reckon, she'll give me some money? . . . I know reading . . . Well. I did once. One night I was down by the steam factory. The warm water runs out there and you can warm your feet up a bit, you see. These big lads was talking about the ragged school in the High Street. They said it was good fun – you had a good laugh, making game of the master, and that, and putting out the gas and chucking the slates about. They said there was a fire there. So I went along to have a warm. They used to give us tea parties and magic lantern shows. I got to like it so I went every night. They was mostly thieves that used to go. Thieving the coal and cutting the ropes off of the ships and selling it at the rag shops. We all used to go thieving after School. While we was waiting for the School doors to open we used to plan where we'd go. I got taken up for thieving coals. But they did reading. I never went back when I come out of prison.

Frederick – aged 12-14

JUMP FOR YOUR LIFE
KEN WHITMORE

First presented by the Unicorn Theatre For Young People at the Arts Theatre, London in 1976.

FREDERICK has a difficult task – to persuade all of us in the world and in the audience, to jump into the air at a given moment, or the world will crash to pieces. He has received this startling information from a mole – who points out that the surface of this overcrowded globe is only held firm by the noble effort of the moles. But this is no longer enough – we must act now before it is too late.

In this opening scene set in a crowded Drill Hall, FREDERICK is pushed on to the stage. He is very nervous – in fact he would be speechless, if the situation of the world were not even more desperate than his shyness. Slowly he gathers confidence despite continued heckling from a disbelieving audience.

Published by Samuel French, London

Frederick

(Into the wings) All right! No need to shove. *(He takes four steps across the stage and stops when he sees the size of the audience. He is momentarily at a loss for words but falls back on his usual greeting)* Hello! How do? *(Pause)* By gumbo, hundreds of 'em! *(Pause)* Can you hear me all right? I'm a bit scared. I didn't expect so many of you. *(He scans the audience from side to side, up and down)* Hundreds of 'em! Hundreds of people who don't believe in the moles. Boys and girls, most of you. Some grown-ups o' course. I'm not surprised they don't believe. But boys and girls. I thought they could work things out – like – more clear. They've sent me here to change your minds for you. The Professor and Mr Harridge and Old Gumbolt. There's a load of people down at the Drill Hall who don't believe in the moles and won't jump at jumping time. That's what they said. Well, it's true. You can bet your life on that. It's true about the moles . . . It is! And if you don't all jump in the air two hours from now the whole world's going to be splintered to bits and we'll all be goners . . . You've got to believe. You've got to jump. Or we'll all go up in smoke. *(Pause)* Listen – you children. *(Pointing to the Hecklers)* Never mind what they say – Laurel and Hardy. At five o'clock tonight we've all got to jump in the air. All at the same time. You and me and everybody in every country and every island and every nation. Everybody. Chinese, Russians, English, Eskimoes – cannibals! All the folk in the world have got to be off the ground at the same split second. So there's not one foot touching the earth anywhere on this planet. Listen, all the grandmas and grandads are going to jump . . . I've got a letter here. *(He takes a letter from his pocket and holds it up)* Mrs Olga Shipoochin, aged ninety-seven, of Moscow. In Russia, that is. You should see all the letters I get. Tons! Now listen to this. *(He reads from the letter)* 'Dear Frederick Kitchener Spudkins,' – that's me – 'We will be thinking of you and jumping with you when the time comes. And my husband Nikolai, who only has one left leg . . . will be jumping as well. All best love, dear comrade jumper.' . . . And there's loads more I could tell you about but there's not the time. There's only two hours left. *(He glances at his watch)* One hour and forty-eight minutes . . . O.K. Tell me this, then. Even if you're right. Even if the moles can't save the world. Even if nothing horrible is going to happen and it's all a – a fantastic fib. What have you got to lose by standing up and giving a little jump, eh? Like this. *(He jumps)* Look. How's it going to spoil your day just to give a little jump? *(He jumps)* Like that.

Jay – a bird

THE SEE-SAW TREE
DAVID WOOD

First performed at the Redgrave Theatre, Farnham in 1986 by the Farnham Repertory Company. The play looks at the world of an oak tree – the See-Saw Tree – and the animals dwelling in and around it, whose lives are shattered by the news that the tree is about to be felled.

In this early scene the Mistlethrush is singing loudly and out of tune – a dreadful noise – when suddenly **JAY** arrives. He is brashly confident, a salesbird supreme. Inside his coat his 'wares' are neatly displayed – dried grasses, quality mosses and badger hair. He carries a suitcase filled with special cleaning materials all ready to sell to his reluctant neighbours – Mistlethrush, Dunnock and Squirrel. He lands on a branch just below Mistlethrush and near to Squirrel's drey.

Published by Amber Lane Press, Charlbury, Oxfordshire

Jay

What music fills my ears? . . . Such tone. Such pitch. Such artistry . . .
Jay's the name, madam. Travelling salesbird supreme . . . I have been on
a flight of exploration, madam, spreading my wings far and wide in search
of marketable merchandise. Scouring the countryside for new and
exciting lines to offer my lucky customers at bargain prices. What do
you fancy? . . . Aha! See my selection, perfect for the use of building
nests. *(He opens his coat. Inside his wares are neatly displayed)* Dried
grasses, bracken, quality mosses, badger hair, sheep's wool for extra
warmth, polythene and paper. Pick your own, mix 'n' match, yours for
the modest sum of two acorns. Can't say fairer than that . . . Do me a
favour . . . Aha! Think ahead, madam. Think of when your eggs hatch.
Think of all those hungry little beaks to feed. No problem. *(He opens
the other side of his coat, revealing more merchandise)* I've got crab
apples, juicy slugs, calorie-stuffed caterpillars, mouthwatering worms,
specially selected spiders, meaty maggots and crunchy moths. Take your
pick . . . Your loss, dear lady, not mine. Happy laying . . . *(He approaches
Squirrel's drey)* Wakey, wakey! Anyone at home? *(Dunnock appears,
carrying rubbish from the drey)* Give a bird a chance, Dunnock! Where's
Squirrel? . . . Cleaning? Aha! Glad you said that. Ideal for the use of.
(He opens his 'suitcase', displaying more wares) Look at this little lot.
Bark scourer, lichen loosener, fungus flusher, mildew stripper, leafmould
remover. Tried and tested. Satisfaction guaranteed . . . I'm only asking
one acorn per item.

Gaspode (A dog)

THE TRUTH
TERRY PRATCHETT

Adapted for stage by Stephen Briggs

First presented by the Unicorn Theatre, Abingdon in November 2000.

Rumour has spread around Discworld that a murder *may* have been committed. William de Worde is their very first investigative journalist, reporting local news and gossip and the appearance of a funny shaped vegetable. But high up in Ankh-Morpork's society dark forces are plotting to overthrow the city's ruler, Lord Vetinari. They've employed two thugs Mr Tulip and Mr Pin who are prepared to carry out any dirty deed. William de Worde is determined to unravel the mystery. The Truth is important. He is helped in his investigation by an informant known only as Deep Bone.

In this opening scene, **GASPODE** is alone on stage. He explains that this is Discworld, where 'magic has a way of bending the rules' and dogs can talk. He introduces the audience to Corporal Nobbs and Sergeant Colon, Foul Old Ron – a smelly beggar and a *mutterer* who is impossible to get away from without giving him money – and finally, William de Worde himself.

Methuen Drama, London

Gaspode

Wotcha. I'm Gaspode. Yes, I know dogs aren't meant to be able to talk, but this is Discworld, where magic has a way of bending the normal rules of science. Our story takes place in the Disc's principle city, Ankh-Morpork. A city so lawless that even the thieves go around in twos. Our story starts with a rumour. It spread around this great city like wildfire – in fact wildfire *itself* has spread through Ankh-Morpork quite a few times since its citizens learned about fire insurance, but I digress . . . *(He looks conspiratorially to left and right)* It even reached the ears of the city's Night Watch. *(He looks up at* Nobby and Colon, *who have entered into a raised part of the stage)* The dwarfs can turn lead into gold . . . (Foul Old Ron *Scraplit. Thatch and trouser. I told 'im. I told 'im. Millennium Hand and Shrimp. Buggrit.)*

Looks like a dirty deed to me, too. *(To the audience)* Oh, sorry – this is Foul Old Ron. One of the city's best-known and most pungent beggars. He is a *Mutterer* – you know . . . he walks behind people muttering until they give him money not to. He's usually accompanied by his Smell, which has become so powerful over the years that it has developed a life of its own . . .

And that's about it for the intro. Ooh, no, sorry, nearly forgot our main character, Mr William de Worde . . . *(The lights come up on William, writing) He* heard the rumour, too . . . and he duly wrote it down. 'Cos that's what he does, see? He writes down rumours and other news in a letter, then sends it to rulers and nobs in other cities and countries so they can keep up-to-date with what's goin' on here in Ankh-Morpork . . . 'Cos he sends so *many* letters, he only actually writes *one*, which he then transfers onto a wooden block and then has it cut into a printing block by Mr Cripslock, the engraver. Then he prints off a wadge of copies, fills in the 'Dear Lady Margolotta's and so on, and everyone thinks he's offerin' a personal service. Clever, eh? And it pays quite well, too.

Eustace – aged 12–13

THE VOYAGE OF THE DAWN TREADER
C.S. LEWIS

Adapted for the stage by Glyn Robbins

The Dawn Treader is a dragon-ship led by Caspian, the young King of Narnia. Caspian has sworn an oath to search out the seven missing Lords, sent out on a dangerous mission across the sea beyond the Eastern Ocean.

In this scene Lucy and Edmund are sitting looking at a picture of a Narnian dragon-ship on the wall. They both miss Narnia – their magic land behind the wardrobe. Lucy knows it is useless to try to get back there. It can only happen when they least expect it. They are interrupted by their bossy cousin, **EUSTACE**. He teases them about Narnia. To him it's a whole lot of nonsense. As the three of them gaze at the dragon-ship, the picture comes to life and they are all drawn into it.

In this scene the three children have been shipwrecked on Dragon Island and **EUSTACE** is alone, bemoaning his fate.

Published by Samuel French, London

Eustace

First, a picture comes to life. Then, I'm half-drowned. Then I'm dragged on board that horrible ship to meet a bunch of real weirdos. I get attacked by a mouse. Then I'm sold as a slave. And finally shipwrecked on this awful looking island. Well, one thing's for sure, I'm never going back on the *Dawn Treader* again. Never, ever again. I hope it's so badly damaged that it never puts to sea again. There must be a British Consul somewhere. There's always a British Consul. Whenever you're in trouble abroad, go to the British Consul. That's what Ma and Pa say. So it must be true. And what about that dreadful storm? I hate the sea. I'd much rather fly. I love flying. It's much safer. And quicker. Why, the crew of that awful ship hadn't even got emergency rockets or a radio to call for help. All they did was yell for Aslan, whatever that may mean. Aslan! Aslan! What a silly name! But at least I've got away from that nasty little mouse. He really hurt me with that spiky little sword of his. Ooh, I can still feel it. I detest that Reepicheep. He's not a mouse, he's a rat. A rotten little rat. Oh, where's this British Consul? What's that over there? It looks like smoke. And where there's smoke, there's fire. That's what Ma and Pa always say. A nice, warm fire to dry me out. And I won't tell the others.

(The smoke is coming from a cave up-stage, *towards which he walks)*

(He stumbles) What's that? *(He bends down, picks something up and rubs it)* It's a coin. A gold coin. Gold! There's some more! Yes, look. Here. And here. And here. And those look like jewels. Look at this beautiful armlet. *(He picks the armlet up and wears it)* Why, the cave is full of treasure. I've found a treasure cave! And finders keepers. It's mine, all mine. Now I'll show everyone who's really in charge. What's that? Ugh! That's disgusting . . .

(EUSTACE disappears into the cave)

Sadie – aged 16, Belfast

ACROSS THE BARRICADES
JOAN LINGARD

Adapted by David Ian Neville

First published in 2003 and set in Belfast in the 1970s at a time of terrible hatred and violence.

SADIE JACKSON is a Protestant. Her friend, Kevin McCoy is a Catholic. Although they live near one another there is an enormous gulf between them – a gulf of prejudice, bitterness and fear. Their friends and families think they should give up their friendship, particularly as Kevin has been beaten up because of their association.

In this scene Kevin's sister, Brede, begs **SADIE** to finish with her brother.

Oxford Modern Playscripts, Oxford

Sadie

I don't know Brede, I don't know . . . I don't know anything at all. I want to see Kevin and he wants to see me and all these people are getting between us . . . Is it right for me to give in to Brian Rafferty and his friends? Is it? . . .

You know, it's funny . . . people say I'm my own worst enemy . . . I make trouble for myself. They say you should go out with one of your own kind . . . it's easier, less aggravation. Well, for goodness sake, you're all missing the point, aren't you? I'm not going out with Kevin because he's Catholic, or a Mick, or whatever you want to call him . . . I'm going out with him because he's Kevin . . . We like being with each other, we don't want to be with anyone else. I mean, I could have met a Protestant and felt the same way about him as I do about Kevin, but it didn't happen like that, did it? If I meet Kevin, he might get beaten up again; if I don't, he'll hate me . . . What sort of choice is that for anyone? I just want a laugh, I want a bit of fun . . . I just want us to be walking out together, just the two of us, sharing things, spending time together . . . Why can't we do that? . . .

It's not much to ask to want to walk by the river with someone you like . . . I'm not sure, I can't promise, Brede. How can I promise never to see Kevin again? I have to think about it.

Gemma – aged 14

JUNK
MELVIN BURGESS

Adapted for stage by John Retallack

First produced by Oxford Stage Company and opened at The Castle, Wellingborough in 1998.

Tar, aged fourteen, is planning to run away from his violent home life. He loves **GEMMA** and begs her to go with him. She comes from a loving home, but her parents are strict. They insist she stays in at night to do her homework and now they have forbidden her to see Tar again. She has always wanted excitement in her life and after a big row with her father agrees to go with Tar.

They join up with friends in a very comfortable squat near St Paul's. At first all is well, but **GEMMA** easily becomes bored. Their friends are older and concerned for the two fourteen year olds. They also have house rules. It's almost like being back with her parents again. Then she meets Lily – her perfect role model.

Lily is the centre of attention wherever she goes. Her clothes are outrageous and so is her behaviour. She invites **GEMMA** and Tar to stay at her place, shows them around the clubs and finally introduces them to Junk.

In this early scene **GEMMA** is sitting at a table on which are laid out relevant items – clothes, sleeping bag, a personal stereo, pen and pencil etc, etc. She introduces the audience to 'Gemma Brogan's practical handbook for running away from home'.

Methuen Drama, London

Gemma

(To audience) Well, here it is – what you've all been waiting for, Gemma Brogan's practical handbook to running away from home. A step-by-step guide:

One. You will need: clothes – woolly vest, plenty of keep-warm stuff. Plenty of underwear and other personal items. A waterproof coat. A personal stereo. A sleeping bag. A pencil and paper. Money. Your father's bank card and PIN number.

Two. Your wits. You'll need 'em.

Three. Think about it. What are your mum and dad going to do? Try to get you back of course. It'll be police. It'll be, oh, my God, my little girl has been abducted. It'll be, maybe some dreadful pervert is at her right now. Maybe she's lying murdered in a bin liner in the town rubbish tip THIS VERY SECOND! It never occurs to them that little Lucinda got so fed up with Mumsy and Dadsy that she actually left of her own accord. So . . . if you don't want every copper in the land on your tail and pictures of you shining out of all the national newspapers, you tell your mum and dad *exactly* what you're doing.

Four. This is where the pencil and paper comes in. You write them a note explaining that you're going away. Wish them luck, tell them no hard feelings and that you hope they will understand.

Five. Book your coach ticket using your father's Visa card.

Six. Go the the cash machine – take the money – and run.

Thank you very much.

Lisa – London, aged 17

THE POWER OF THE DOG
ELLEN DRYDEN

First performed at the Orange Tree Theatre, Richmond in 1996.

Vivien Chadwick, Head of the English Department in a failing school run by an incompetent Headmaster, is preparing to take up a new appointment as Head of a school in South London. At the same time she is attempting to move house as well as visit her mother who has had a stroke,

Added to these problems is **LISA**, a brilliant but difficult sixth former, who she is encouraging to stay on at school and try for a place in university. In this scene Vivien is in her study waiting for **LISA** to arrive for an extra tutorial. **LISA** turns up late as usual with the same old excuses – waiting thirty-five minutes for the bus and Mum being stroppy. Vivien asks if there is any chance of Mum coming to see her.

Published by First Writes Publications, London

Lisa

Nah! She doesn't like schools. Give her panic attacks. *(Pause)* And I don't want you to come to my house . . . *(LISA turns her back. Then changes the subject with great energy)* Listen. I reckon you owe me ten quid. I went to see that *Midsummer Night's Dream*. It was rubbish! Helena was about thirty-five, kept chucking herself all over the place – tossing her hair back and flinging her arms about. You know – just like young people always do when we're in love. Nearly ruptured herself. She was about six inches shorter than Hermia as well, so she'd got these gross high heels and Hermia had to bend at the knees all through the quarrel scene. And the Mechanicals wandered about in the audience and talked to us. I hate that! And Peter Quince sat in the Stalls and shouted his lines from there. And the fairies all lived in cardboard boxes and had tattoos. Puck was a drug-pusher. And it went on for nearly four hours. I reckon ours was better. And I couldn't afford it! . . .

Hey and guess what! Theseus and Hypolita played Oberon and Titania! Isn't that original? Everybody liked it except me. I wanted to get up and kill them all. Bunch of no-hopers . . . I really love that play . . . I don't think this had any . . . respect. And it wasn't – magic . . . *(She stops, lost in thought for a moment)* I know. 'The best in this kind are but shadows and the worst no worse if imagination amend them . . . It must be your imagination then and not theirs.' *(She is very still. Her face becomes a mask)*

(Very quietly) I like – magic. *(Briskly)* I suppose I'm talking rubbish – everybody else says it's brilliant. And they're paid to be in the imagination business, aren't they? And I've got no right to criticize them.

Martha – Yorkshire
THE SECRET GARDEN
FRANCES HODGSON BURNETT
Adapted for the theatre by Thérèse Kitchin

First performed at the Farrer Theatre, Eton in 1990 and then at the Wilde Theatre in 1995 by the Quercus Theatre Company. The action takes place in 1911.

Young Mary Lennox has been sent from India to live in her uncle's big house in Yorkshire. Her uncle, a strange withdrawn man, wants nothing to do with her and leaves her in the charge of his stern housekeeper, Mrs Medlock and **MARTHA** – a young servant girl. **MARTHA** is sorry for Mary and does her best to cheer her up. She encourages her to play out in the grounds, and it is here that Mary finds an old walled garden that has been locked up for years. She asks the gardener about it, and is told not to 'poke her nose where it's no cause to go'.

In this scene she begs **MARTHA** to tell her the story of the secret garden and reluctantly **MARTHA** explains that it had once belonged to her uncle's young wife who died ten years ago.

Published by William Heinemann Ltd, Oxford

Martha

Mrs Medlock says it's not to be talked about. Mrs Medlock says his troubles are nowt of his servants' business. Tha'lt get me into trouble . . . I'll lose my place here, then what'll mother do . . . If it weren't for garden – he wouldn't be as he is . . . She made it her own – none of t'gardeners was ever let in . . . Him an' her they looked after it themselves . . . They'd shut t'door an' stay there for hours – laughin' an' talkin' . . . as though it were a world of their own . . . They planted roses – wild, climbin' things – He built her a swing – an' she fashioned a seat in t'branch of old tree . . . Even now I want to cry . . . The bough broke an' she fell to the ground . . . Mother says she was just a slip of a thing most likely teasin' him from up there in the tree . . . She was hurt so bad that soon after she died . . . If she hadn't been as she was – she might have got better . . . There's lots of things that are not to be talked of in this place . . . Anyway – that's what happened and he nearly went mad an' he's never recovered . . . You musn't tell Mrs Medlock what I've told you . . . Promise . . . An' now tha'lt be a good child an' not try to wander where tha's not meant to go. Tha's better off than some. Mother says you ought to be learnin' thy books, an' tha' ought to have a woman to look after you. Mother says, 'You just think how you'd feel, Martha, shut up by thee sen in a big place like that with no other . . . You do your best to cheer her up.' So I brought thee a present . . . *(Holds out skipping rope)* What is it for! Does tha' mean they've got no skippin' ropes in India for all they've got elephants and tigers. This is what it's for . . . *(She skips . . . stopping)* I could skip longer than that. I've skipped as much as five hundred when I was twelve – you have a try . . . It'll tire you out, then you'll sleep an' not bother about wind howling!

Viola – young

TWELFTH NIGHT
WILLIAM SHAKESPEARE

The first performance noted was in 1602 and the play was published in 1623.

VIOLA and her twin brother, Sebastian, have been shipwrecked in a storm off the shores of Illyria. They are separated and VIOLA, believing her brother to be drowned and unable to live without finding work, disguises herself as a pageboy and finds employment in Duke Orsino's household.

She is sent by her master to deliver messages and love tokens to the Lady Olivia, who is not in the least bit interested in him. VIOLA by now has found herself falling in love with the Duke, but cannot declare her love as he believes her to be a boy.

In this scene, VIOLA is on her way back to the Duke, having delivered his latest message to Olivia. She is stopped by Olivia's steward, Malvolio, who throws a ring at her feet declaring, 'My lady wants none of your Lord's ring!' VIOLA realises that Olivia has fallen in love with her, just as she herself has fallen in love with the Duke. Neither of them can do anything about it and she realises her disguise has been a terrible mistake.

Penguin Classics, London

'proper false'	handsome but false, well-looking but deceitful
'fadge'	turn out
'thriftless'	useless
'pregnant'	receptive or clever, ingenious, artful

Viola

Malvolio *exits*

I left no ring with her: what means this Lady:
Fortune forbid my outside have not charm'd her:
She made good view of me, indeed so much,
That sure methought her eyes had lost her tongue,
For she did speak in starts distractedly.
She loves me sure, the cunning of her passion
Invites me in this churlish messenger:
None of my Lord's ring. Why he sent her none:
I am the man, if it be so, as 'tis,
Poor Lady, she were better love a dream:
Disguise, I see thou art a wickedness,
Wherein the pregnant enemy does much.
How easy is it, for the proper-false
In women's waxen hearts to set their forms:
Alas, our frailty is the cause, not we,
For such as we are made, if such we be:
How will this fadge? My master loves her dearly,
And I (poor monster) fond as much on him:
And she (mistaken) seems to dote on me:
What will become of this? As I am man,
My state is desperate for my master's love:
As I am woman (now alas the day)
What thriftless sighs shall poor Olivia breathe?
O time, thou must untangle this, not I,
It is too hard a knot for me t' untie.

Exit

The Grand High Witch

THE WITCHES
ROALD DAHL

Adapted by David Wood

First performed at the Lyceum Theatre, Sheffield in 1992 and then at the Duke of York's Theatre, London.

The Witches are holding their annual meeting at the Hotel Magnificent, Bournemouth, under the cover name of The Royal Society of the Prevention of Cruelty to Children. The meeting is presided over by the **GRAND HIGH WITCH,** who having removed her wig and mask – revealing a wizened, horrible, rotting face – proceeds to lay out her plan to 'rub out' all the children of England within a year.

Published by Samuel French, London

Grand High Witch

You may rrree-moof your vigs, and get some fresh air into your spotty scalps. [The Witches *reveal their bald heads*] Vitches of Inkland. Miserrrable vitches. Useless lazy vitches. You are a heap of idle good-for-nothing vurms! . . . As I am eating my lunch, I am looking out of the vindow at the beach. And vot am I seeing? I am seeing a rrrevolting sight, which is putting me off my food. Hundreds of rrrotten rrrepulsive children. Playing on the sand. Vye have you not got rrrid of them? Vye? . . . You vill do better . . . My orders are that every single child in Inkland shall be rrrubbed out, sqvashed, sqvirted, sqvittered and frittered before I come here again in vun year's time . . . Who said that? Who dares to argue with me? [She points dramatically at Witch Two] It vos you, vos it not? . . . Come here. [She beckons. Witch Two, mesmerised, ascends the platform]

> A vitch who dares to say I'm wrrrong
> Vill not be vith us very long!
>
> A stupid vitch who answers back
> Must burn until her bones are black!

[Staring at Witch Two, the GRAND HIGH WITCH gestures. Sparks fly. Smoke rises – Witch Two disappears] I hope nobody else is going to make me cross today. [She finds the smouldering remnants of Witch Two's clothes and holds them up] Frrrizzled like a frrritter. Cooked like a carrot. You vill never see her again. Now vee can get down to business . . . I am having a plan. A giganticus plan! . . . You vill buy sveetshops . . . You vill fill them high vith luscious sveets and tasty chocs! . . . You vill have a Great Gala Opening with free sveets and chocs for every child! . . . You vill be filling every choc and every sveet vith my latest and grrreatest magic formula. [She produces a potion bottle] Formula Eighty-Six Delayed Action Mouse-Maker! . . . To cause delayed action, rrroast in the oven vun alarm-clock set to go off at nine o'clock in the morning . . . Inject vun droplet of the formula in each sveet or choc, open your shop, and as the children pour in on their vay home from school . . . [She chants]

> Crrram them full of sticky eats,
> Send them home still guzzling sveets,
> And in the morning little fools
> Go marching off to separate schools.

Ronnie

CHICKEN SOUP WITH BARLEY
ARNOLD WESKER

First produced at the Belgrade Theatre, Coventry in 1958 and later transferred to the Royal Court Theatre in London. Part of *The Wesker Trilogy*, this is the story of an East End family and their gradual disillusionment as one by one their ideals slip away from them. The early part of the play covers the period before the Second World War, with the excitement over the Spanish Civil War of the thirties and the anti-Blackshirt demonstrations. Then, later, we see the characters devoting their energies towards the creation of a new world.

In this scene it is October 1947. **RONNIE**, now a teenager, is listening to the wireless and conducting an imaginary orchestra, when his Aunt Cissie lets herself into the house. She asks him if his father is still working in the same job.

Published by Methuen Drama, London

Ronnie

No, he's a store-keeper in a sweet factory now. Look. *(Shows her a biscuit tin full of sweets)* Jelly babies. Can't help himself. Doesn't do it on a large scale, mind, just a handful each night. Everyone does it . . . You know he can't stay long at a job – and now he has got what he has always wanted – a legitimate excuse . . . He walks – slowly and stooped – with his head sunk into his shoulders, hands in his pockets *(Imitates his father)*. His step isn't sure – frightened to exert himself in case he should suddenly drop dead. You ought to see him in a strong wind – *(Moves drunkenly round the room)* – like an autumn leaf. He seems to have given up the fight, as though *thank God* he was no longer responsible for himself. You know, Aunt, I don't suppose there is anything more terrifying to a man than his own sense of failure, and your brother Harry is really a very sensitive man. No one knows more than he does how he's failed. Now that's tragedy for you: having the ability to see what is happening to yourself and yet not being able to do anything about it. Like a long nightmare. God! fancy being born just to live a long nightmare. He gets around. But who knows how sick he is? Now we can't tell his lethargy from his illness . . . Here! *(Goes to a drawer and takes out a notebook)* Did you know he once started to write his autobiography? Listen. *(Reads)* 'Of me, the dummy and my family.' How's that for a poetic title! 'Sitting at my work in the shop one day my attention was drawn to the dummy that we all try the work on. The rhythm of the machines and my constant looking at the dummy rocked me off in a kind of sleepy daze. And to my surprise the dummy began to take the shape of a human, it began to speak. Softly at first, so softly I could hardly hear it. And then louder and still louder, and it seemed to raise its eyebrows and with a challenge asked: your life, what of your life? My life? I had never thought, and I began to take my mind back, way back to the time when I was a little boy.' There, a whole notebook full, and then one day he stopped! Just like that! God knows why a man stops doing the one thing that can keep him together.

Loll – Gloucestershire

CIDER WITH ROSIE
LAURIE LEE

A stage adaptation by James Roose-Evans

Performed at the Hampstead Theatre in 1963 and later transferred
to the Garrick Theatre, London. The poet, Laurie Lee – known as
LOLL to his family and friends – looks back on scenes from his childhood in a Cotswold village.

In this scene he remembers a family picnic, with his mother, the
children from her husband's first marriage, Marge, Doth and Phyll
and his two brothers, Jack and Tony. Phyll asks their mother to tell
them about their uncles. **LOLL** reminds them of Uncle Sid and the
time he got the sack from the bus company.

(*Note* In the play the Narrator, Laurie Lee, is played by an adult actor
remembering his childhood self. The young Laurie Lee is played by
a young actor. However, for the purpose of this extract I have joined
their two speeches together. Also note the characters were origi-
nally played in Gloucestershire accents but as an audition speech
this is a matter of individual choice.)

Published by Samuel French, London

Loll

Our Uncle Sid was the best double-decker bus driver in Stroud, without doubt, even safer, more inspired when he drank. Everybody knew this, except the bus company. He began to get lectures, admonitions, stern warnings, and finally suspensions without pay. When this last happened, out of respect for our Aunt Alice, he always committed suicide. Indeed, he committed suicide more than any man I know. But always in the most reasonable manner. If he drowned himself, then the canal was dry. If he jumped down a well, so was that; and when he drank disinfectant there was always an antidote ready, clearly marked, to save everyone the trouble. He reasoned, quite rightly, that Aunt Alice's anger, on hearing of another suspension, would be swallowed by her larger anxiety on finding him again so near to death. And Auntie Alice never failed him in this and forgave him each time he recovered. The bus company were almost equally forgiving, they took him back again and again. Mam, do you remember the time when the bus company gave Uncle Sid the sack for good? . . . They found him asleep at the wheel – he were drunk! And that night, we were sitting by the fire when there was a knock at the door. It were Auntie Alice and the girls. They were all dressed in black. 'He's done it this time,' she said, 'He's gone off to end it all. He's gone to Deadcombe Wood. He always told me he would!' And then she turned to our Mam and said, 'Oh, Nance, Nance, he'll do himself in. Your boys, they just got to find him.' So Jack and I put on our coats and we went up the valley, towards Deadcombe Wood. It were raining. We beat up and down through the wood, calling 'Uncle, Uncle!' We were real scared. We didn't know what we might find. We were about to go home when suddenly we saw him. He were standing on tiptoe under an oak tree with his braces round his neck, looped to a branch. The elastic made him bob up and down! He were in a terrible temper. Do you know what he said? *'You've been a bloody long time!'*

Nathan – mid teens

LITTLE SWEET THING
ROY WILLIAMS

Premiered at the New Wolsey Theatre, Ipswich in 2005.

NATHAN is a white boy in his mid-teens with a good future ahead of him. Football is his life and already Arsenal are interested in him. Tash is a black girl, also in her mid teens. She acts tough but underneath is a sensitive loving girl. Her brother Kev has just come out of prison and is trying hard to make a better life for himself as they all three struggle to survive the pressures of the local gun culture.

NATHAN is fond of Tash and she likes him, although she persists in taunting him.

In this scene he is kicking a football around. He is extremely skilful but misses a shot as Tash enters. She teases him, and he tells her how he saved the match last week, scoring two goals in seventy seconds to beat the Christopher Wren team.

Methuen Drama, London

Nathan

Enter NATHAN *and* Tash.

(NATHAN *is kicking his ball about. He is very skilful. He misses a shot)*
Have a go. Come on, try it. See how far you get without me getting it off yer . . .

We beat Christopher Wren last week . . . Four-two! . . . Two-one down at half-time, we were, me on the bench . . . Mr Cotton reckoned I'm doing too much, reckons I still need a break. A change of attitude is required, he says. Semi-finals of the cup, ain't won it in years, mega-game, Christopher Wren ain't soft, best team in the borough. I'm well up for this, so well up, and he leaves me on the bench, 'cos he wants to change my attitude, does that make sense to you? . . . Bloody stupid, I reckon. Well, he found out when we were two-nil down in the first five minutes. Cotton is a fool, he don't know what day it is. His tactics are all wrong, does he listen? Bring back –

(Tash – Mr Singh.)

Chris Wren are a mouthy lot as well . . . Listen to me . . . From two-one down, we were three-two ahead by the fiftieth minute. I scored two in seventy seconds . . . First, I fed Danny Lopez the ball, he pushed up, I followed, he then laid a pass for me to prod home . . .

Before anyone knew it, I was on the ball again, fifty yards out. I glided past one defender, around another, then I guided my shot in the far corner as the last two defenders crashed into each other. Ten minutes later, I was at it again, headed the ball in with this wicked cross from Liam. Finally, last minutes of the game, Tony Sadler played a beauty ball forward, my first shot was blocked by the keeper but it bounced back off him, all for me, easy tap! . . .

See? . . . I told you I knew what I was talking, told you I knew what I was doing. You got nuttin' to say to me on that, Tash. You can't touch me on that.

Hally – South African

'MASTER HAROLD' . . . AND THE BOYS
ATHOL FUGARD

Performed at the Market Theatre, Johannesburg in 1983 and later that year at the National Theatre in London, the play opens in the St George's Park Tea Room on a wet and windy Port Elizabeth afternoon in 1950. **HALLY**, a young white South African boy, son of the tea-room proprietess, has just got back from school. Sam, a black waiter in his forties, fetches a towel for him to dry his hair. **HALLY** has always been closer to Sam than to his own parents, and in this scene **HALLY** remembers the time Sam made a kite for him.

From: *Athol Fugard – Selected Plays*, published by Oxford Paperbacks, Oxford

Hally

It started off looking like another of those useless nothing-to-do after-noons. I'd already been down to Main Street looking for adventure, but nothing had happened. I didn't feel like climbing trees in the Donkin Park or pretending I was a private eye and following a stranger . . . so as usual: See what's cooking in Sam's room. This time it was you on the floor. You had two thin pieces of wood and you were smoothing them down with a knife. It didn't look particularly interesting, but when I asked you what you were doing, you just said, 'Wait and see, Hally. Wait . . . and see' . . . in that secret sort of way of yours, so I knew there was a surprise coming. You teased me, you bugger, by being deliberately slow and not answering my questions! (Sam *laughs*) And whistling while you worked away! God, it was infuriating! I could have brained you! It was only when you tied them together in a cross and put that down on the brown paper that I realised what you were doing. 'Sam is making a kite?' And when I asked you and you said 'Yes' . . . *(Shaking his head with disbelief)* The sheer audacity of it took my breath away. I mean, seriously, what the hell does a black man know about flying a kite? . . . When we left the boarding house to go up onto the hill, I was praying quietly that there wouldn't be any other kids around to laugh at us . . . Can you remember what the poor thing looked like? Tomato-box wood and brown paper! Flour and water for glue! Two of my mother's old stock-ings for a tail, and then all those bits and pieces of string you made me tie together so that we could fly it! . . . You went a little distance from me down the hill, you held it up ready to let it go . . . 'That is it,' I thought. 'like everything else in my life, here comes another fiasco.' Then you shouted, 'Go, Hally!' and I started to run. *(Another pause)* I don't know how to describe it, Sam. *Ja!* The miracle happened! I was running, waiting for it to crash to the ground, but instead suddenly there was something alive behind me at the end of the string, tugging at it as if it wanted to be free. I looked back . . . *(Shakes his head)* . . . I still can't believe my eyes. It was flying! . . . It was sort of sad bringing it down, Sam. And it looked sad again when it was lying there on the ground. Like something that had lost its soul. Just tomato-box wood, brown paper and two of my mother's old stockings! But, hell, I'll never forget that first moment when I saw it up there. I had a stiff neck the next day from looking up so much.

The Artful Dodger

OLIVER TWIST
CHARLES DICKENS

Written in 1838, this is the story of a young orphan, Oliver, who runs away to London and meets up with another boy, Jack Dawkins, known as the **ARTFUL DODGER**. The **DODGER** introduces Oliver to the sinister Fagin, who runs a Thieves Den, sending out young boys to pick the pockets of the rich.

In this scene, Oliver is on his knees cleaning the **DODGER**'s boots for him, while **DODGER** explains the advantages of joining Fagin's gang. Although the **DODGER** is young and only four foot six tall, he has all the airs and manners of a man about town.

Dodger

(Sighs and resumes his pipe) I suppose you don't even know what a prig is? . . . I am. I'd scorn to be anything else. So's Charley. So's Fagin. So's Sikes. So's Nancy. So's Bet. So we all are, down to the dog. And he's the downiest one of the lot! He wouldn't so much as bark in a witness-box for fear of committing himself; no, not if you tied him up in one, and left him there without wittles for a fortnight. He's a rum dog. Don't he look fierce at any strange cove that laughs or sings when he's in company! Won't he growl at all, when he hears a fiddle playing! And don't he hate other dogs as ain't of his breed! – Oh no! He's an out-and-out Christian . . . Why don't you put yourself under Fagin, Oliver? And make a fortun' out of hand? And so be able to retire on your property, and do the gen-teel; as I mean to, in the very next leap-year but four that ever comes, and the forty-second Tuesday in Trinity-week . . . Go! Why, where's your spirit? Don't you take any pride out of yourself? Would you go and be dependent on your friends ? . . . Look here. *(Drawing forth a handful of shillings and halfpence)* Here's a jolly life! What's the odds where it comes from? Here, catch hold; there's plenty more where they were took from . . . You've been brought up bad. Fagin will make something of you, though, or you'll be the first he ever had that turned out unprofitable. You'd better begin at once; for you'll come to the trade long before you think of it; and you're only losing time, Oliver . . . If you don't take pocket-handkerchers and watches, some other cove will; so that the coves that lose 'em will be the worse, and you'll be all the worse too, and nobody half a ha'p'orth the better, except the chaps wot gets them – and you've just as good a right to them as they have.

Tony Lumpkin – aged 17–20

SHE STOOPS TO CONQUER
OLIVER GOLDSMITH

This 18th century comedy was first produced at the Theatre Royal, Covent Garden, London in 1773. It is set in the Hardcastles' country mansion and parodies the sentimental comedies popular in that time.

The action revolves around the arranged match and courtship between the Hardcastles' daughter, Kate and Young Marlow, and the practical jokes played on family and friends by **TONY LUMPKIN**, Mrs Hardcastle's son by a former marriage. **TONY** has been ordered by his mother to marry his cousin, Constance, but he wants nothing to do with her. When he discovers she is in love with Marlow's friend, Hastings, he is only too delighted to help the lovers elope together. His mother discovers the plot, and insists on accompanying Constance to her Aunt Pedigree's home 30 miles away. **TONY** takes charge of the coach journey, driving them round and round the neighbouring countryside, finally tipping everyone into the local duck pond. Here he describes the adventure to Hastings, whose only concern is for Constance's safety.

New Mermaids

circumbendibus	roundabout process
cattle	stable slang for 'horses'
draggled	dirtied by being dragged through wet mud
quickset hedge	a hedge formed of 'quick' – i.e. living – plants

Tony

Left them? Why where should I leave them, but where I found them?
. . . Riddle me this then. What's that goes round the house, and round
the house, and never touches the house? . . . Why, that's it, mon. I have
led them astray. By jingo, there's not a pond or slough within five miles
of the place but they can tell the taste of . . . You shall hear. I first took
them down Feather-bed Lane, where we stuck fast in the mud. I then
rattled them crack over the stones of Up-and-down Hill – I then intro-
duced them to the gibbet on Heavy-tree Heath, and from that, with a
cicumbendibus, I fairly lodged them in the horsepond at the bottom of
the garden . . . No, no. Only mother is confoundedly frightened. She
thinks herself forty miles off. She's sick of the journey, and the cattle
can scarce crawl. So if your own horses be ready, you may whip off with
cousin, and I'll be bound that no soul here can budge a foot to follow
you . . . Ay, now it's dear friend, noble Squire. Just now, it was all idiot,
cub, and run me through the guts. Damn *your* way of fighting, I say.
After we take a knock in this part of the country, we kiss and be friends.
But if you had run me through the guts, then I should be dead, and you
might go kiss the hangman . . . Never fear me. Here she comes. Vanish.
She's got from the pond, and draggled up to the waist like a mermaid
. . . *(Enter* Mrs Hardcastle] Alack, mama, it was all your own fault. You
would be for running away by night, without knowing one inch of the
way.

Sebastian – young

TWELFTH NIGHT
WILLIAM SHAKESPEARE

The first performance was noted in 1602 and the play published in 1623.

SEBASTIAN and his twin sister, Viola have been shipwrecked. They are separated in the storm and each imagines the other to have drowned.

Viola is washed up on the shores of Illyria and having no money or means of buying food, disguises herself as a pageboy, Caesario, and finds employment with Duke Orsino. She is sent to deliver love messages to the beautiful Lady Olivia, who has no interest in the Duke, but falls helplessly in love with his young page.

The problem is solved when **SEBASTIAN**, accompanied by his Sea Captain friend, Antonio, arrives in Illyria, determined to find out what has happened to his sister. Left on his own, he wanders by chance into the Lady Olivia's garden. Olivia greets him fondly and thinking him to be her love, Caesario, presses a pearl into his hand saying, 'Keep this for me.'

In this scene a bewildered **SEBASTIAN** is examining the pearl and wondering if he has indeed gone mad.

Penguin Classics, London

Sebastian

Enter SEBASTIAN.

This is the air, that is the glorious Sun,
This pearl she gave me, I do feel't, and see't,
And though 'tis wonder that enwraps me thus,
Yet 'tis not madness. Where's Antonio then,
I could not find him at the Elephant,
Yet there he was, and there I found this credit,
That he did range the town to see me out,
His counsel now might do me golden service,
For though my soul disputes well with my sense,
That this may be some error, but no madness,
Yet doth this accident and flood of Fortune,
So far exceed all instance, all discourse,
That I am ready to distrust mine eyes,
And wrangle with my reason that persuades me
To any other trust, but that I am mad,
Or else the Lady's mad; yet if 'twere so,
She could not sway her house, command her followers,
Take, and give back affairs, and their dispatch,
With such a smooth, discreet, and stable bearing
As I perceive she does: there's something in't
That is deceivable. But here the Lady comes.

Enter Olivia *and* Priest.

Useful addresses

The Actors' Theatre School
Evening classes and private tuition
32 Exeter Road
London   NW2 4SB
Tel: 020 8450 0371
Fax: 020 8450 1057

Offstage Bookshop
Website: www.offstagebooks.com
Email: offstagebookshop@aol.com
Mobile: 07970 582529

The British Library
96 Euston Road
London   NW1 2DB
Tel: 020 7412 7677 (*Reader Admissions*)

Victoria Library
160 Buckingham Palace Road
London   SW1W 9UD
Tel: 020 7641 4287

London Academy of Music and Dramatic Art (LAMDA)
155 Talgarth Road
London   W14 9DA
Tel: 020 8834 0521

Copyright holders

Fantastic Mr Fox by Roald Dahl, adapted by Sally Reid. Reproduced by permission of David Higham Associates Limited. Published by Penguin, London.

Extract from *Flibberty and the Penguin* by David Wood is reproduced by permission of Samuel French Ltd, 52 Fitzroy Street, London W1T 5JR to whom applications for performance should be made.

The Giraffe and the Pelly and Me. © 1995 Roald Dahl Nominee Ltd & Vicky Ireland. Adapted from Act I, scenes 1, 2 & 3. Published by Samuel French, London. All rights whatsoever in this play are strictly reserved and application for performance etc., must be made before rehearsal to David Higham Associates Ltd, 5–8 Lower John Street, Golden Square, London W1F 9HA. No performance may be given unless a licence has been obtained.

Have You Seen Zandile? by Gcina Mhlophe, Maralin Vanrenen and Thembi Mtshali. Published by University of KwaZulu-Natal Press.

In Service by Ellen Dryden. Taken from *Six Primroses Each and Other Plays for Young Actors*. Reproduced by permission of First Writes Theatre Company Ltd. Published by First Writes Publications, London.

Invisible Friends by Alan Ayckbourn. Reproduced by permission of Faber & Faber Ltd. Published by Faber & Faber Ltd, London.

James and the Giant Peach by Roald Dahl, adapted by Richard R. George. Reproduced by permission of David Higham Associates Ltd. Published by Penguin, London.

Jump For Your Life by Ken Whitmore. © Ken Whitmore. Reproduced by permission of The Agency (London) Ltd. First published by Samuel French 1980. All rights reserved and enquiries to The Agency (London) Ltd, 24 Pottery Lane, London W11 4LZ info@theagency.co.uk

Junk by Melvin Burgess, adapted by John Retallack. Published by Methuen Drama.

Extract from *Kindertransport* by Diane Samuels. Published by Nick Hern Books.

The Lion, the Witch and the Wardrobe by C.S. Lewis, dramatised by Adrian Mitchell. Reproduced by permission of Oberon Books Ltd. Published by Oberon Books, London.

Little Sweet Thing by Roy Williams. Published by Methuen Drama.